Homeschooling

How to Painlessly Start a Homeschool Program

(All You Need to Create the Best Curriculum and Learning Environment for Your Child)

Jorge Marin

Published By **John Kembrey**

Jorge Marin

All Rights Reserved

Homeschooling: How to Painlessly Start a Homeschool Program (All You Need to Create the Best Curriculum and Learning Environment for Your Child)

ISBN 978-1-7780617-9-0

No part of this guidebook shall be reproduced in any form without permission in writing from the publisher except in the case of brief quotations embodied in critical articles or reviews.

Legal & Disclaimer

The information contained in this book is not designed to replace or take the place of any form of medicine or professional medical advice. The information in this book has been provided for educational & entertainment purposes only.

The information contained in this book has been compiled from sources deemed reliable, and it is accurate to the best of the Author's knowledge; however, the Author cannot guarantee its accuracy and validity and cannot be held liable for any errors or omissions. Changes are periodically made to this book. You must consult your doctor or get professional medical advice before using any of the suggested remedies, techniques, or information in this book.

Upon using the information contained in this book, you agree to hold harmless the Author from and against any damages, costs, and expenses, including any legal fees potentially resulting from the application of any of the information provided by this guide. This disclaimer applies to any damages or injury caused by the use and application, whether directly or indirectly, of any advice or information presented, whether for breach of contract, tort, negligence, personal injury, criminal intent, or under any other cause of action.

You agree to accept all risks of using the information presented inside this book. You need to consult a professional medical practitioner in order to ensure you are both able and healthy enough to participate in this program.

Table Of Contents

Chapter 1: The Goals Of Middle School.... 1

Chapter 2: How To Benefits 8

Chapter 3: The Possibility Of Success 19

Chapter 4: Effective Strategies To Get Things Doing 34

Chapter 5: Middle School Teaching English 43

Chapter 6: Reading Liste 58

Chapter 7: Mathematics And Science 69

Chapter 8: Teaching Other Middle School Topics 73

Chapter 9: In The Future High School And Beyond... 83

Chapter 10: Produce A Short Film 91

Chapter 11: Design The Fairy Trail.......... 99

Chapter 12: Take A Trip........................ 113

Chapter 13: Organize A Dinner Party ... 123

Chapter 14: Put Your Money Into The Stock Market.. 136

Chapter 15: The Year That Changed Everything.. 146

Chapter 16: Does It Make Sense To Home School My Children? 150

Chapter 17: What Is De Schooling And Game Schooling? 163

Chapter 18: What Is The Learning Style Of Your Child?.. 169

Chapter 19: There Are Many Different Styles 176

Chapter 1: The Goals Of Middle School
Education for Students

Middle school marks the break between high school and elementary school. The children learn differently -- not just those who are homeschooled, but everyone! The pause in middle school provides those who struggle or are reluctant to learn time to catch up in preparation for graduation. While at the same time the pause gives fast and well-educated children the opportunity to keep learning on their own level.

The primary goal of a middle school program is to offer students who need of some help with their math. students who aren't at grade level in math may be able to concentrate on math. The time can be used to get up to grade. One of the advantages of the middle schools is that it's virtually impossible to get in the back of the class. If your child isn't at their grade, then middle school's purpose is to assist them in reaching the grade they need to be at. It's not your fault or your kid is in the right place.

The other goal is to provide those students that are at or above grade level an opportunity to progress directly into high school activities. Students who have completed high school proficiently and employing high school curriculum who have a good grasp of the material, could earn early high school credits for their school transcripts. Algebra 1 biology and foreign language are the most common courses at the high school level that teachers teach during the middle elementary school.

Certain children are on the right track at their grade. Some children don't need remedial help or have the ability to take advanced classes. The child does not have to complete the remedial work or even high school It is possible to let them complete remedial work in a specific area, go towards high school in others but remain at the their grade for the remainder of the time.

Your responsibility is to instruct your children to their ability throughout every day. You child could be at an academic level but struggle with math or be a pro at a foreign language yet struggle in maths, despite the other subjects being on track. The best part of homeschooling is the ability to meet your child's needs academically throughout the curriculum.

Middle school is an opportunity when your child can be taught something unfamiliar. They must learn to study, and be more independent and responsible. They should begin becoming responsible for their learning.

Many parents believe that the very first day of seventh grade, their kids will be self-sufficient and accountable. If that's the case then you'll find yourself disappointed. The transition to independence isn't sudden It happens over a period of time in intervals and then it ends. Children can be self-sufficient on one occasion and completely unresponsible one day and completely responsible the next. Be patient. Similar to the hormonal changes that influence an individual's mood day to day, this is applicable to their independence.

Girls and boys alike Independence and responsibility are not an easy path. It's not without its moments of highs and lows. It's not easy; as parents, you don't be sure what type of child you'll awake to each day.

Parenting Purposes

The main reason for middle schooling parents is studying how to teach high schools. That is the job you have to do. Home education is your chosen vocation. It is essential to put in the time. Make sure you are taking part in ongoing education so that you don't accident and burn in the time of your high school. Know what you should learn so that you are not be in a panic.

It's not just about investing in your child's education and your family, but also for yourself as well as your homeschool. Attend classes on homeschooling high school, and take business trips for parents of homeschool children to go to a convention for homeschoolers. Participate in parent education courses on the internet, study books on high school and purchase books on college admissions and scholarship. All of this will allow you to pay for college, and will assist your child to go on to a life after homeschoolingfor college and into a job.

Middle school is the ideal opportunity to get started on the benefits of homeschooling in high school. Find out what you are afraid of and then make yourself more knowledgeable. If you're afraid about teaching algebra, you are able to educate yourself on algebra, and also the many different courses offered.

Discover more about high schools when your child is in middle school. This is a period of training for you and not your final test. This is your chance to improve your homeschooling skills.

The job of a parent is to not be worried. The fear of going to high school is often what prompts parents to give up school at home. Don't let fear rule your life. Learn more about yourself so that you are able to make educated decisions concerning your child's destiny, instead of based on fear. The power of knowledge is. Learning the basics of middle school and high school can help you overcome your anxiety so that you are able to take a more informed choice. Find out more about the subject to help you improve your confidence over time.

Another reason for parents of homeschool children is to develop the skills of record keeping. Learn about keeping records before your children start high school. Make great records and move ahead in confidence. This will allow learners to grow without chance of failing.

Keep records like your child attended the high school. Start working on transcripts as well as writing out the course description. Discover the types of attendance record homeschoolers need to keep within your state. This can help you avoid panic as you prepare for high school. To learn more about recording, you might like to read my book Setting the Records Straight. The book describes the best way to store the records, and how to create transcripts and courses descriptions.

Chapter 2: How To Benefits

The advantages of homeschooling won't end after your child has finished the elementary school. There are many advantages to having your middle school children homeschooled.

Social Benefits

The most significant advantage of homeschooling in at middle school lies in the enduring connection it creates between parents and children. Parents who homeschool from this point often see an enormous change in their relationships and their child.

As homeschool parents spend a lot of time with their children They can change to, shape, and mold their behaviour. They also learn to fall in love with in time. Once you have started with homeschooling, the relationship will smooth out while you work out the balance between normal and extraordinary at home. The children can come up with their own views and have conversations of the highest caliber about recent events, morals and beliefs. These discussions are essential for your children when they are growing into adults.

Another reason to homeschool in middle school can be the superior interactions your child is able to have. At both private and public schools, kids are subjected to forced socialization based solely on their age. Socialization in the real world happens in the context of your child living in the home with their family and is socializing freely in the local community. If they have a positive experience of socialization this can help build confidence in them.

It's also a safe and secure environment to help your child's education, and free of the fear of being bullied. In the absence of the school environment, your child in middle school will be able to have fun with friends, without being judged or laughing because they're taller, shorter and fat or scrawny.

At middle school, kids attempt to determine who they are going to become. Do they want to be rude, or will they be pleasant people? In the early years, children tend to want to be good people. When they are to high school, they will decide which kind of person they would like to be: good or not.

Middle school students are constantly moving between classes which is where the issue lies. Between one school day and another, they aren't sure what they can expect from one their fellow classmates. The best person they have today might turn out to be an awful girl the next day. It's a tense time that it could be a very difficult period in a child's lives as they are surrounded by youngsters who haven't determined if they'll be good or bad.

One of the biggest advantages of homeschooling a middle school is having the chance to mold and influence your child's behaviour every day. Children this age have hormones that are rushing through their body. They are able to go from awe-inspiring to angry within 60 minutes or lesser. It's a good idea to help them understand that it's fine for them to let their hormones be a mess however it's not acceptable to speak rudely around their mommy. It is important to help your children learn what is acceptable conduct, no matter what they're being.

Certain middle schoolers appear like they're in the elementary school. Others middle schoolers appear to be more mature teens. One of my kids was always on the lower end of the scale, and seemed younger than his age due to his short height. Another son of mine was tall in comparison to his age, and was a slightly more athletic. So it was like an average middle schooler. My kids had a good acquaintance who was tall and broad shoulder He was like an 18-year-old at when he was at middle school. This difference in maturity could be a challenge.

It's the same in terms in academics. Students have a wide range of abilities at middle high school. This isn't your fault or your fault that puberty occurs earlier. It's not your fault that you have triggered an earlier maturity rate, since you can't manage it.

The same is true for the way you raise your child isn't accountable for the amazing achievements of your child also. It all has to have to do with the physical development, as the body's hormones control the process of physical development and maturity.

Physical Advantages

It is possible to adapt to any hormonal changes that the child has to face. Changes in the body of your child freaks their parents out. As a result of the rush of hormones the way they behave can change. The maturity of their physical and academic abilities will shift. Intellectual and maturation rates differ. It's impossible to influence the situation. However there's lots that you can do to help your child during the changes.

If you have a child who's physically mature, you have the time needed in teaching her to take look after her body. It is possible to teach her about beauty in her and make sure that both boys and girls aren't sulking at her due to the physical maturation. Make sure that you're safe in your her home (because the 18-year old boy could believe she's an 18-year-old).

When your physically less developed child ages, you may explain to them that various maturity levels are not unusual. When they are at home, they do not need to think about changing to P.E. before 30 or 40 others and getting ridiculed for their physical insanity.

Character Benefits

It is possible to instill values and ethics into your child, to assist them in learning how to improve and grow so they will be able to impact the world instead of being in the hands of others. In the six years between high school and middle school You strive to create an adult that can be an inspiration and a lighthouse and change the world to improve the lives of all mankind. If they are exposed to the news you see on the evening news prior to them being mature enough, it could cause them to fall completely out of the water.

The situation is changing due to the rise in social media. There is a sense that the negative news and happenings around the globe are frequent and widespread that teens are convinced that they live in an ominous world. The world of social media isn't always full of high-quality ethics. Middle school is a very vital time to help children increase their faith as well as knowledge of what is the difference between right and right and wrong. Your influence is less on your children when they reach middle school years, and begin to develop a firm belief system. You can influence your child as much as you are able to.

You can provide an education appropriate to your personal beliefs and values. While doing this you're able to promote the passion for education. Education in the public sector is increasingly placing been focusing on unsuitable education that is not in any way connected with literacy, but all to do with general social morals which you might or not be a fan of.

As the parent in charge of your child's education, you are able to ensure that it is appropriate the child's age. A proper middle school education implies that you teach them the fundamentals that they can build upon over the next four years of high school. They should be able to comprehend and read for the secondary schooling year.

Family Benefits

There will be a growing sense of growth in independence for your kids. As they grow more self-sufficient, you will be able to provide them with the skills that will help them succeed in adulthood. Not only are they home-schooled and growing up at home, but also learning too.

It's not like you could drive by your child's home with a vehicle packed with tools for adults and then dump everything on them all at all at. Instead, provide tools in a systematic manner, one step at a time to ensure your child doesn't get overwhelmed with adult responsibility. Encourage your child to learn responsible behavior in tiny doses.

A third benefit for families is the joy of spending time as a family. While you are homeschooling it means you are at home as a family a lot more often. Family time is a chance to bond as well as have time to enjoy entertainment during the course of the day.

Middle school aren't easy as it's a period that there is less freedom in our finances. The summer holidays we took were usually at home, and these are the moments that I will remember the most fondly. Things you can do with your family like camping, walking through the city, eating dinner as well as family gatherings are all great ways to build a relationship with your loved ones that can last as you grow older.

It is the time that children are separated from their families, grow up, and later onto become part of a family that includes their partner. Make time to create lasting family memories so that when they are been separated from their family, they can remember the affection of their parents and other siblings. If they're ready for it to return to visit you, become part of your family as they move forward in an extended family group in bliss for many years to come.

Trouble Solving Together

Another reason to homeschool middle school is that it gives you the chance to work together on problems and tackle challenges head-on. There are ethical, difficult issues that families have to are constantly confronted with. It is common to see stories in the news that are difficult to you or your morals, as well as the beliefs you hold.

If you are homeschooling middle school, it is possible to tackle these issues with your children. When your children are struggling with their behavior, get into trouble, or are misbehaving or are even experimenting using alcohol or drugs You can tackle the issues at home with them.

Chapter 3: The Possibility Of Success

Create a well-organized study area and have all the tools you need on the ready. Make sure you have a spot to save documents, perhaps even an individual notebook per topic. Instruct your child to study using a plan or an assignments list, and also to utilize an assignment calendar. If they know a set location, time as well as a procedure to study Children are more likely to carry good studying practices with them into college.

Help your child learn how to organize their tasks. The most effective approach is to complete what's "worst initially." It is possible to tackle those that are the most challenging or interesting topics initially. It can also help reduce large tasks into small stages and determine how long every step takes.

Four Tips for Organising Your Middle School

1. Be a Purposeful Learner Everyday

It is important for your child to take their time learning every day. This doesn't necessarily mean knowing how to utilize formulas in the spreadsheet. It's a sign that you are teaching your kid something that they do not know. It is easier to learn on purpose by using a rigorous curriculum and attending classes that require a lot of effort.

2. Make use of challenging, but not overwhelming Instructional

The word "challenging" means that your child is required to give it a go. It doesn't mean that you have to do it all at once. Be careful not to ask your child excessive amounts of time or effort. It is impossible for them to succeed if you're demanding excessive time or difficult. Be sure to not overburden your classes or curriculum in order to allow them to succeed.

3. Make good habits

This could be a problem to parents who think they're lacking good behavior. It's your goal to raise responsible adults, even if you're not feeling like one, you should continue to work on educating your child to establish healthy behaviors. If you're not a very well-organized person, this is the perfect opportunity for both you and your child how to build good habits with each other.

4. Offer Your Child an Annual Review

An annual test is required in a lot of states. Some states make it an option and parents may not like the notion of an annual exam. An annual exam could help middle schoolers in two ways.

An annual evaluation can help you determine where your child's academic progress is. Are they doing better than their peers? Do they have a disadvantage? Are there any aspects of their education they've left out you must be aware of?

An annual exam allows your child to get familiar using exams. As they grow, they'll older and will be required to take the SAT exam, ACT test, or an exam for drivers, and you do not wish for them to be unable to concentrate and be frightened by stress over the test. Give your child a relevant annual assessment of their grade is often a great way in understanding your child as well as help them understand the process of taking tests.

and Time Management. and Time Management

Homeschooling in elementary school is encouraging your child to be active, have fun and be exposed to learning. As they enter Middle School, it is important to need to provide them with an awareness of the adult realm of time management and scheduling while letting them be excited about studying at the same time. This is the perfect time to instruct, motivate to practice and teach managing time and organizing.

Skills for organizing don't come by magic. There is no way to turn a knob and see your 7th grader quickly organized and awake with an alarm clock. The opposite occurs because the preteen's sleeping needs are so intense that it's hard for them to get up without an alarm.

Learn and practice organizing and time management skills. Explore different scheduling options and get children to provide feedback. No matter what time you do math prior to noon or at noon. Plan assignments and reserve the time for each subject.

Certain moms excel in scheduling, and they know many years ahead of time which projects they're planning to work on. Others families aren't capable of how far ahead they can plan but that's okay as well. It is possible to study math at 9 am and history at ten each morning. If they allow a specific time limit for each course, they can receive the same amount of homework done.

Moreover, their kids still receive an education, and are equally productive.

In middle school, when I was homeschooled I experimented with a range of different methods for scheduling. I was able to set up a single day-by-day schedule. I also attempted the weekly plan. After that we went on to give our children the entire week in one glance. The idea was to give them a non-binding timetable for the week. They soon realized they wouldn't be able to get the task done if delayed it until the Friday on a weekly basis.

No matter which option you decide to do. Choose a schedule that suits the best for your child and you.

Learning to Teach Study Skills Help your children to be aware of their time obligations and be sure that the expectations are fair when they have to balance with their friends and school.

Encourage children to study regularly. can be the most beneficial. Make sure they don't have to cram on tests or composing papers in the last moment which can happen when working in classrooms and co-op environments.

Give students assignments to finish their work independently as they develop time management skills. Offer them one each day for a while at the beginning. After that, you can begin to assign tasks for one week each day. In high school, a bit later the child should be prepared for assignments that span a long time maybe one month at one moment.

It is helpful to have a schedule to help the child learn about adult work as well as high school assignments along with college classes and work in the field. It is possible to get them used to working on tasks that require to be finished in a time-bound manner.

Instruct them to utilize the calendar in order to keep track of their tasks and other activities. Some kids love calendars. Learn to teach your child how to utilize a calendar with the basis of.

Aid your child in learning to complete their work on time. While doing this it is important to be flexible. Teachers are also flexible and you ought to as well. Keep a healthy balance and encourage pupils to complete their work within the timeframe, however remain flexible in the event that something unexpected occurs.

Instruct your children in the method of working on the worst first. The weakest region is what they focus on throughout school hours in order to remove it from the way. First, they must perform the job and after that they're free to play to play. This can assist your child build a solid attitude to work and be more productive in the world of work.

Encourage your child to have breaks during their studies. I would suggest 30-50 minutes of studying followed by a 10 minute break. This is particularly essential for students who are active or young men as well as athletes. Regular breaks for exercise will help adolescents manage hormones.

It's unhealthy to be seated in front of a computer for hours. Kids must take a break and stretch their legs, body, stretch their minds and forget about their the work. This is like taking a breathing in and then taking a bite of a cracker in between sips of cheese. The children need breaks to let them go on.

The idea of taking a break doesn't seem to be a natural thing for children. It is possible for them to be somewhat unfocused and think they'll never finish their math homework and feel the need to show a sense of perfection or a desire to complete it. There's a time when there's declining marginal return, specifically in math subjects and math. A child will only solve a limited amount of math questions until the brain is unable to perform math any more. Be sure that your child has regularly scheduled breaks for study.

Don't allow your child to take cram exams or delay writing essays at the last minute. You must educate your child with care. If you are a homeschooler it's not any issues when it comes to cramming test questions, however, it is possible when children attend classes outside of at home or within co-op. Concentrate upon the main reason you homeschool learning and have fun -- and not to memorize for tests.

Help your child take exams calmly and with no anxiety and for the best performance. It can be difficult for children who are having difficulty finding their feet and dealing with stressful situations in a calm manner. Make sure to maintain an unflinching, calm and objective approach to taking tests.

This is similar to teaching courage. My children were taught the importance of bravery when I explained that it may involve crying. It's appropriate to cry when doing something courageous. Being brave is taking the steps you have to take on.

I would suggest that you teach your children to take tests similar to how you train your kids about visiting the doctor. There is nothing to stress out about. You may experience some discomfort at times and it can be helpful over the long term. Middle school is the best opportunity to instruct this.

The goal is to help children reach an independent level at the time they're ready. The curriculum varies according to subject and also by child. in truth, it differs in terms of curriculum.

Six Mistakes to Avoid

1. Don't Expect Instant Maturity

Children appear to look like they're 8 years old, while other children appear as though they're 18. Do not expect all of them to be mature in the same way or behave maturely simultaneously, not at all on a daily basis.

2. Don't expect consistent behavior

The moods of middle schoolers and hormones change. Positive and negative moods are common to all of us. Therefore, we should not expect uniform behaviors from our children. It is our goal to mold and shape their behaviour so that they are more mature and capable of altering their behavior as they would in adulthood regardless of how they're being.

3. Beware of expecting learning styles to change

Parents are of two minds. kids reach seventh grade, they must immediately begin to use the textbooks as bees would to honey. But it's not the way the way they learn remains the same. Boys who are active and wiggly remain active, the wiggly eighth and seventh graders. Girls who are shy will remain timid. Find a program which allows your child to play by playing math, and allow your auditory child to learn about science and historical.

4. Don't Expect Complete Independence

Children don't lose their independence in a flash. This isn't how they work. Learn to teach your kids self-reliance and get to get a new task.

5. Don't Be Comparative -- Someone Might Get Hurt

There is always a risk of injury as parents become involved in comparing. It's never been more apparent than when you are in middle school in which some children are maturing early while others mature later -- only a few grow up "on the right time."

6. Don't have unreasonable expectations

It's always good to determine if you're putting in too much effort or doing too little. Are your children doing more every day than you'd have the ability to do? Do you expect your child as more responsible than you?

Keep your child's pace

You can expect gradual, slow-changing adjustments that are gradual and slow. Take a look at the differences between a baby's birth and a toddler. This didn't happen in a flash; it required 2 years.

You can expect your middle schooler to alter their stops and start like a baby. They lay down and inactive for a long duration. In a flash you'll see them begin walking and then the next morning they're moving.

Changes in behavior will occur gradually with a child in middle school as well. They'll suddenly be responsible on one issue, but will not be accountable for something other.

Be mindful. Take your time and follow the child's progress.

The preparation for life

Middle school homeschooling is about preparing students for the future. Let your child become the best prepared possible, so they will be able to use the talents God gave them to improvement of the society.

Help your child learn to read, write and talk with confidence. Help them learn math efficiently, precisely and effortlessly. That's your aim to ensure that your kids are ready for the future.

Chapter 4: Effective Strategies To Get Things Doing

Middle school is the ideal time to increase and enhance your child's reading skills. Literacy is the ability to read, write and math. Writing must be legible, and you must spell effectively or else they won't be considered to be proficient. If you come across people at the market who cannot make money out and cannot read their checks, they're considered illiterate.

It is your responsibility to improve and increase your child's reading to ensure that when they turn adult, they're prepared to become a part of the community. The rate of progress is not the same for everyone.

A child might have severe difficulty reading, or may have difficulties in writing words with three letters. A different child may be reading famous Jane Austen novels in middle school. The two children have the same needs. Be sure to help your child move through the steps of the ladder toward literacy by taking each step one at a time, and avoid forcing them to jump at the very top of the eight-foot ladder. It is possible that they fall down yet again, and end up hurting their own bodies.

Writing, reading as well as math comprise the three components of literacy. They are the core disciplines. Science and social studies are also essential classes. Apart from these fundamental courses, you'll also find the study of foreign languages, critical thinking art and Bible classes.

Develop Positive Habits

One of the most effective fundamental strategies is to develop positive routines. Create study habits and learning skills to help guide your child into the high school level and on into adulthood. Learn to teach yourself by introducing a small amount at a.

Every 15 minutes my children were at work I was beyond thrilled. They were 15 minutes of tranquility and I was able to finish my laundry. The process starts by allowing 15 minutes of freedom each moment. The transition will be gradual.

You're who is responsible for home education Your child must follow your instructions. Students should finish their assignments with no complaining.

Help your child understand integrity so they will never lie or deceive anyone. There is a possibility for homeschoolers to commit a crime; it's rare and yet it happens. Make sure you check on your child regularly on a daily schedule. It's hard to spot any cheating that occurs day-to-day. If you keep track of your child at a daily appointment every single day or at least three to four every week, it will be obvious when they're cheating because it's apparent.

A good habit is to do chores. Young children are members of the family along with students. Give some chores of the household to the youngsters. Every year, they will grow more responsible and accountable, not just for homeschool chores, but also for chores at home.

An Array of Normal

There's an array of middle school students. You can expect a range of skills. There are some students who stand out. They are gifted, or academically proficient because they're motivated. Some students face challenges within a single or several aspects. There's no wrong you could do as an adult parent of a student in the middle grade. Let them be where they are within the normal limits of their abilities.

Remedial Learners

It's difficult when you have to deal by a child having a difficult time learning. The level of maturity of a child and their ability to learn differ. Brains may not be able to perform tasks that it doesn't have the synapses to perform, like creating sentences. This could also be the result of the result of a learning impairment, like dyslexia.

The first step is to focus on diverse methods of learning. Consider if you can satisfy your child's requirements by adjusting their learning style with a method that is more logical to their brain. For those who are auditory learners you can begin by distributing oral reports or engaging in discussions rather than writing assessments (especially in cases where writing is an issue). If your child is finding difficulty reading, try the audio or video method of instruction.

As well as conversations, think about sharing your thoughts with others as it is a popular approach used to assist students who are struggling in the private and public schools. It's possible to do it as well. Your child will receive exactly what they want.

Let them move while teaching. This can be extremely beneficial for youngsters who have trouble getting their bodies to move around to understand. Studies show that students who learn kinesthetically cannot learn when they're moving. Do not sit down with your child at a desk, without allowing them to tap their feet or pencil or move their legs or arms.

Every child learns more if they are they are forced to sit at a computer. Children benefit from moving. Some things are just enough to boost the capacity of your child to be a better learner. Some children find coloring during an audiobook or watching a movie could be beneficial. Other children find being seated and playing with the exercise ball while working in their classes or solving math-related tasks helps them to learn. One of my kids had been in high school we let him play on an indoor trampoline while he was learning math terms. He was able to absorb them better than he would had without the movement.

Concentrate on transferring information to and the student's mind in the quickest way possible. Do not try to squeeze the square peg to fit into an oval hole. Don't scold your child over their shortcomings; instead, teach them your child to use their strengths.

Make sure you get the facts out quickly as you can. If your child has a knack for taking tests testing could be beneficial. If your child is a bit more mature, discussions and projects or creating videos could be better.

In the case of learners who are struggling for whom remedial learning is not an option, it may be useful to differentiate academics from interactions with others. If your child suffering from severely dyslexia is required to read aloud in a group class and feels like they are insignificant as well as incompetent. Be sure that the time spent with friends is for fun, and not a time for the academics.

It is also possible to differentiate your child's disability in learning from the other subject areas. You shouldn't be requiring studying in the fields of science or history to your child suffering from dyslexia. They can read to them, listen to audio books and even watch videos. Be sure not to force your child suffering from dysgraphia to be able to write every single thing. Focus on the area of difficulty, for instance writing or reading, however do not work at it all the time throughout the day and your child could get angry and will eventually become apathetic to study.

Learn to tackle difficult subjects separately. Work at the child's level, so that they feel like they're learning something However, not too much that they get overwhelmed. Don't require too much.

It is possible to get assistance for your learners who are struggling. Problems are often made visible when children are in the middle of school. One of the first places to find help is to consult your doctor. It's not always as difficult as a visit to your eye specialist. Children are often found to suffer from a learning impairment however all they require is glasses.

Participate in homeschool events and look for an expert in your area. If you're unable to go to an event, look on the website of the convention to find out the presence of any specialist and then look up their contact info.

Chapter 5: Middle School Teaching English

When it comes to middle-school, you will find an array of different. It is your responsibility to teach your child's needs at the appropriate ability level. In planning the middle school curriculum take into consideration what you'll have to cover and how you will teach your enthusiastic or recalcitrant student. Be sure to keep each class according to your child's level of ability. Don't be concerned if your child's grades are in the back, because that's what middle school is all about It's an opportunity to improve or speed up.

Writing and reading are the foundation of literacy, and the capacity to be a student. There are some kids who don't have to be pushed. Others require for you to be mindful of what you do to encourage the reading.

How do you motivate readers in the middle schools? Let me list the methods! Inspiring children to read can be an enjoyable way of helping youngsters enjoy their education. If reading is fun and enjoyable, kids view that homeschooling is a rewarding education option instead of an obligation imposed on them by a teacher. Find ways to make reading more enjoyable by using these easy-to-implement suggestions.

Seven Tips to Encourage Reading at Middle School

1. Create a Cozy Corner

At home, the comfortable corner was wherever the dog would hide. In the couch, or under the sun's rays, spending time reading with pets can create the feeling of comfort and comfort that kids learn to connect with reading. There are pillows and blankets. Many parents have a place to sit close to a bookcase that is filled with amusing and age-appropriate books.

Create a comfy space outside to accommodate a nervous young child. Set up a hammock in the yard's corner or in a covered area over your deck so the child can rock around while they read. Rocking chairs can help students who require kinesthetic learning and move while they read.

2. Style a Bedroom Paradise

When children grow older, they could abandon their reading space and prefer to devote more time to their bedrooms. It is possible to create an environment and a routine that promotes the reading of books on their own.

Take away any technology in their rooms in the first place, so that they can play instead of reading. Create bedtime reading guidelines and also a light-out time. Choose a fun or fashionable reading light or headlamp to use with your child. After that, they can be reading until they are tired and shut off the lights and not get out of bed. Do not let them read on electronic devices as it could impact their sleep.

3. Offer an Yummy Dessert Some adults (like myself!) like to drink their cup of coffee while they read the newspaper every morning. Other adults prefer to read books while sipping tea. The kids can have the similar comfort food. Serve cookies and cocoa. be simple, or make a traditional teatime such as the Tuesday Teatime recommended by Brave Writer, incorporating discussion as well as poetry alongside your desserts. Enjoy tea or coffee in beautiful cups and saucers during your teatime to be special.

4. Improve Fluency through Fluff

When your kids are able to read, their next thing to do is to increase their vocabulary, ability, speed and fluency. While reading books that are challenging can help improve vocabulary the most however, it is possible take a different direction to encourage children to read fast. It is possible to increase their efficiency and speed by letting children read at a lower of reading.

It is possible that my kids have been spending long hours in front of Calvin and Hobbes comics However, the comics helped inspire them to learn quickly. Take care to review the comics you offer as they've changed in the last few years. It is possible to use better quality books, but of course the books are below readers' levels. Since reading gets easier it will allow them to read more quickly and be more confident.

5. The focus should be on discussion, not the Confrontation

You can snuff out the passion for reading in a child's mind when you study and analyze every piece of literature. It's not required or suggested to conduct literary analysis on each piece of literature that you have read.

Make reading enjoyable by abstaining from comprehension worksheets whenever you can. Instead of asking tests-style questions often have a discussion open to all on the strengths of a book, and then share thoughts about it with your children. The constant analysis of literature can lead kids to conclude, "This must be school" rather than "I enjoy reading."

6. Brainstorm Tie-in Activities

In lieu of formal analyses alternatively, try other activities that are more entertaining. You can play games that tie into the story. Children can also play out stories using puppets or Lego figurines. Search online for activities that are great to read classic literature. There are recipes you can bake, suggestions for field trips as well as hands-on activities and movies to watch.

A few families gather for the purpose of forming a book group. It could be run as a easy, with everyone making a brief presentation on why they enjoyed the book (or wasn't) and what they think others ought to read the book (or should not). It's a bit the public speaking part however you can create a fun experience for kids who just want to gather together and have fun with sweets.

As a homeschooler the kids, we would gather at an eatery that served pizza. Each child was given a speech, and they were given a certificate for a customized size pizza. My children were very excited through pizza and it was an enormous achievement for the entire family of homeschoolers.

7. Beware of reading the wrong Books

Give real books (not books for school reading) featuring high quality storytelling and excellent writing. Children may say that they do not like reading. This could be due to the fact that they are reading inappropriate books! Find titles that appeal to their interests by focusing on their favorite topics.

Explore different types of non-fiction as well as fiction. Look at magazines, non-fiction about the subjects they study to learn by delight, or classic graphic novels like Tintin of Tibet. Anything that will encourage children to read is a great concept. Reading that is enjoyable will make reading more fun for them. It's true that you do not desire them to only read nonfiction and graphic novels all the time However, offering a diverse range of titles will allow children to enjoy reading.

Things to avoid

Don't force your child to take a reading course and immediately giving them a test about the book. There is a way to engage in a debate rather, particularly in the event that you've read the book ahead of time yourself. Have a conversation with friends. Think about presenting oral talks which include discussions instead of conflict.

Beware of book reports whenever possible. It is not necessary to have them given for each book that is that is read. If you have a child who is an avid reader, it could be more report on books! Five to five reports a year would be adequate for most children.

Beware of tests whenever you can. Ruth Beechick wrote in her book"Yes You Can Homeschool in a way that is independent for grades 4-8 that tests is a measure of what a child may not understand. Tests include questions that somebody has come up with and it measures whether your child is able to answer the questions. There could be fifty questions left off the test, but which your child knows the answer to. Testing is a way to determine the things your child doesn't have, discussion will show that your child is able to already know.

Also, it is important to stay away from the schoolbooks. Authors of high quality do not compose grade school reading and teachers who might have trouble writing can be the authors. They conform to the requirements of public schools as well as the needs of public schools. If you select a book of high quality rather than (award winners, for instance) You can be sure they're written well.

One study examined the comparison of a Grade-level reader with the Newberry Medal winner. The participants opened a randomly selected page from every book. For the reader for grade levels they circled all passive verbs which indicate inadequate writing (such as "was" or "was"). There was no passive verb within the Newbery Medal winner. They highlighted many passive words in the readers. It is generally advisable for your child to be exposed to high-quality literature.

It is helpful to have diverse books across genres. There's a wide selection to choose from such as mystery books such as historical fiction, action novels, fantasy novels as well as other genres!

Be aware that your child might like totally different books from what you. I'm not a fan of reading C.S. Lewis' The Lion, the Witch, and the Wardrobe or J.R.R. Tolkien's The Hobbit. My kids loved the books, and they couldn't stop reading them.

Solutions for Rehabilitation Readers

Confidence and competence is the aim. The child must feel that they can read proficiently. It is sometimes necessary to steer clear of reading books that create the feeling of being inadequate. Do not read books on a class if your ability may not be quite at the level you would like to.

Middle schoolers may have read Jane Austen books, but it doesn't mean that you should let your child read them. The child you are raising may not be at the right level for these books. The reading of books that are beyond their capabilities could make them feel like they are not enough.

Encourage them to improve their reading skills through letting them take a break and read a bit of fluff. Like I said that I allowed my kids to go through Calvin as well as

Hobbes comics. They laughed all the way through the comics. I was sure they had good abilities to comprehend reading since they laughed at suitable timings. My friend suffers from severe dyslexia, and was always reading "Popular Mechanical" magazines. The vocabulary of him and his speed was increased even though his mom was not able to get him the reading of a book.

One approach to begin can be to start by reading the initial three chapters in a book in front of your child. The book introduces the child to the words used by the author and provides an understanding of style and character. They will as well be excited to continue studying to find out the next chapter. Beginning a novel can be intimidating for those who are not able to read. If you can begin the book with them, going through the three first chapters aloud, you will assist them in becoming productive.

If you're dealing with an uneasy reader, pick short classics. You can have them read a book within a week, and then do you realize it's smaller than other books. In the case of a child who is dyslexic consider audiobooks so they will be able to read along. If you have a child who is kinesthetic It is useful to look for books with characters who are active. An example of a high school book featuring an active main character can be found in The Adventures of Tom Sawyer.

Writing

Make writing practice a part of your daily routine. It could be as simple as using a pen or using the computer every single day. It is important to ensure that you teach penmanship, and that your child's writing can be read. The penmanship doesn't have to follow the same style just legible enough that others are able to be able to read the text.

Perhaps you would like to add narration exercises as writing assignments during Your English class. Ask your child to explain what they read to you in their own phrases. Your child could take a page from the book, and then write your narration. They'll explain the story using their own words, so you know what they learned from the text.

It is worth considering adding dictation in the mix as well. It was extremely useful for me especially once I got up to teaching punctuation and writing style. I picked paragraphs or sentences from the best writing we were reading. After that, I read the passage in front of my children, and they had them write the passage down. They read it slowly, and transcribing it using the correct punctuation, grammar, as well as spelling. This gave them a sense of what a high-quality piece of literature looks as on piece of paper.

Spelling and Grammar

Incorporate games that help improve your child's language. For spelling, I often recommend Spelling Power. It covers second through 12th grade, meaning you just need to purchase an spelling program only once. In the end in this Spelling Power book, you are able to find games that you can use for all learning styles. If you're a kinesthetic student You'll discover game concepts for example "write one word that fills the entire whiteboard" as well as "write one word spelling with shaving cream and a sheet of cookie."

The learners in Kinesthetics have to be able to be able to move large muscle groups. The movement of their fingers isn't enough as they must be able to move their entire arm. That's why spray painting or sidewalk chalk with water coloring can be far better spelling games instead of writing the word 100 times on a piece paper.

Chapter 6: Reading Liste

It can be difficult to locate suitable books for middle schoolers. If you've got a slow reader, try short classic books. If you have a child who is kinesthetic, concentrate on novels with lively protagonists. If you're a reader who is fervent then feed them by reading quality books instead of books that are merely junk. My children were in this group and were awestruck by reading! When they finished reading an installment of Little House books, I made them read the entire collection. Our family's photo of a homeschooling young boy reading a book, while sitting in front of a pet.

If your child is moody, stay away from darker characters or themes, as well as find books that are positive with heroic characters and triumphant heroes.

The reading lists of middle schools are becoming more sombre in the education system. To get a fascinating look at the analysis, check out the article, Middle

School Reading Lists 100 years ago and. today. A resource that we relied on to help us select titles were The Read Aloud Handbook, written by Jim Trelease. If you're looking for excellent books suitable for students in high school or youngsters who are beyond their age take a look at my College Bound Reading List for ideas!

This list of recommended books is based on widely recommended titles for middle schoolers and heavily influenced by the studying we've done in our home with our kids. If you're unfamiliar with a title on this list, make sure you read the book prior to reading it. It's been quite a while when I've had the chance to read them as a parent of a child in the middle school as the only person who can determine the level of maturity your child has reached.

A word of caution Every family is unique and have to set their own criteria for publications their children will read. Parents take full responsibility in their child's education. If you're not familiar of a topic on this list, make sure you read the text first.

Here are some fantastic titles for middle schoolers aged 11-13. If you want a printable and clickable reading schedule, refer to seven strategies to promote Reading during middle school Reading.

Adams, Richard Watership Down

Alcott, Louisa May An Old Fashioned Girl

Alcott, Louisa May Little Women

Alexander, Lloyd Prydain Chronicles

Angleberger, Tom Origami Yoda Book Series

Auer We Hope That You'll Hear a Cry from Egypt

Auxier, Jonathan The Night Gardener

Babbit, Natalie Tuck Everlasting

Barrie, J.M. Peter Pan

Batson, Thomas Wayne The Door Within series (Christian allegory)

Bendick, Jeanne Galen and the Gateway to Medicine

Bendick, Jeanne Galen Archimedes as well as Jeanne Galen Archimedes and the Door of Science

Berquist, Laura M. The Harp, and the Laurel Wreath

Black, Chuck The Kingdom Series (6 books)

Blackmore, R.D. Lorna Doone

Blackwood, Gary The Shakespeare Stealer

Bolt, Robert A Man for Every Seasons

Bradley, Alan Flavia de Luce series

Bunyan, John Pilgrim's Progress

Burnett, Frances Hodgson The Secret Garden

Carroll, Lewis Alice in Wonderland

Carroll, Lewis Through the Looking Glass

Cather, Willa My Antonia

Chesterton, G.K. "The Ballad of the White Horse

Cody, Matthew Powerless

Cohen, Barbara Seven Daughters and Seven Sons

Collier, James Lincoln My Brother Sam Is Dead

Cummins, Maria Susanna and Baym Nina The Lamplighter

Cushman, Karen Catherine, called Birdie

Dagherty, James The Magna Charta

Dashner, James The Maze Runner series

Decamillo, Kate Tiger Rising

Defoe, Daniel Robinson Crusoe

Di Angeli, Marguerite The Door in the Wall

Dickens, Charles A Christmas Carol

Doyle, Arthur Conan The Redheaded League

Duprau Jeanne Duprau, Jeanne Book of Ember series

Ellis Deborah The Breadwinner (3 books in the series)

Farley, Walter The Black Stallion series

Fitzgerald, Jon D. The Great Brain

Fletcher, Susan The Shadow Spinner

Forbes and Esther Johnny Tremain

Frank, Anne Diary of an Early Girl

Freedman, Russell Freedom Walkers The History of the Montgomery Bus Boycott. Montgomery Bus Boycott

George, Elizabeth The Witch of Blackbird Pond

George and Jean Craighead My Side of the Mountain

George, Jean Craighead Tree Castle Island

Golding, William Lord of the Flies

Gipson, Fred Old Yeller

Graham, Kenneth The Wind through the Willows

Hale, Shannon The Goose Girl

Henty, G.A, Freedom's Cause

Holling, Clancy Paddle to the Sea

Hunt, Irene Across Five Aprils

Jacques, Brian Redwall Series

Jenkins, Jerry B. and LaHaye Tim left Behind: The Kids series

Jewett, Eleanore M. The Hidden Treasure of Glaston

Johnson, Lois W. The Viking Quest series

Juster, Norton The Phantom Tollbooth

Keith, Harold Rifles for Watie

Kipling, Rudyard Captain Courageous

Kipling, Rudyard The Jungle Book

Konigsburg, E.L. The Mixed Up Files of Mrs. Basil E. Frankweiler

L'engle, Madeleine A Wrinkle in Time series

Lawrence, Caroline Roman Mystery series

Lee, Harper To Kill an Mockingbird

Lewis, C.S. The Chronicles of Narnia

Lindgren, Astrid Pippi Longstocking

London, Jack Call of the Wild

London, Jack White Fang

Lowry, Lois The Giver

Lowry, Lois Number the Stars

MacDonald, George The Princess as well as Goblin. Goblin

MacLachlan, Patricia Sarah Plain and Tall

McAllister, M.I. The Mistmantle Chronicles

McCaffrey, Black Horses for the King

McGraw, Eloise Jarvis The Golden Goblet

Montgomery, Lucy Anne of Green Gables series

Moody, Ralph The Dry Divide

Morris, Gerald The Squire's Story

Mull, Brandon and Dorman, Brandon The Fablehaven series

Myers, Walter Dean and Miles, Bill The Harlem Hellfighters

Naylor, Phyllis Reynolds Shiloh

Orwell, George 1984

Orwell, George Animal Farm

Paterson, Katherine Bridge to Terabithia

Paulsen, Gary Hatchet

Pearson, Ridley The Kingdom Keepers: Disney After Dark

Peretti, Frank E. The Cooper Kids Adventure series

Polland, Madeleine Beorn the Proud

Pope, Elizabeth Marie The Sherwood Ring

Pyle, Howard Men of Iron

Pyle, Howard The Story of King Arthur and His Knights

Pyle, Howard Otto of the Silver Hand

Pyle, Howard and McKowen, Scott The Merry Adventures of Robin Hood

Rawlings and Marjorie Kinnan Yearling

Rawls, Wilson Where the Red Fern Grows

Robinson, Barbara The Best Christmas Pageant Ever

Rogers, Jonathan The Wilderking Trilogy

Sewell, Anna Black Beauty

Shafer and Ruth Jashub's Journal

Speare, Elizabeth George The Bronze Bow

Stewart, Trenton Lee The Mysterious Benedict Society

Stevenson, Robert Louis The Black Arrow

Stevenson, Robert Louis Kidnapped

Stevenson, Robert Louis Treasure Island

Sutcliff, Rosemary The Roman Britain trilogy (The The Eagle of the Ninth)

Thom, James Alexander Follow the River

Tolkien, J.R.R. The Hobbit

Chapter 7: Mathematics And Science

Learn math daily. You want to master the subject however, not absolute perfection. Everyone makes mistakes in math at times. Do not expect your child to be flawless However, you should wish for them to be able to comprehend the basics of math.

I would encourage you to incorporate mathematics games that are fun to play in your homeschooling. My personal favorite book for math games to this age group can be found in Family Math: The Middle School Years. It has games to help you learn about algebra.

It is also possible to add greater enjoyment in math through making use of readers. The www.LivingMath.net website has a list of readers to aid in the reinforcement of math concepts for children who are avid readers. They also help inspire reading among children who enjoy math.

Math is usually a terrifying area for parents. It could be the very first topic you're looking for instructional videos. If this occurs be calm as everyone eventually goes to a stage when they're unable to do math. Keep in mind that this is a part of educating your children to be independent learners. Video tutorials are an excellent option.

If you choose to utilize an instructional program, be sure to include student preferences into your the curriculum. Your students' preferences will delight you. It was a bit surprising to me the math textbook my children selected. I love math books that have illustrations, however they did not. Similar is the case with instructional videos. There are kids who have strong opinions concerning the manner in which the instructor appears like, for example. Be sure to watch an example tutorial together with your child prior to purchasing a product.

There is a possibility that your kid earn high school math credit. If your child studies

Algebra 1 or higher level math at middle school, the credits could be included on the transcript of high school.

Science

When you are in middle school, the aim is to make science enjoyable. It is important to instill an interest in learning and make your child enthusiastic about the subject of science. Inspire curiosity, so that they will get a textbook to get excited about science when they enter high school. Instead of reading textbooks in middle school, do units of study. It is also possible to incorporate other activities like looking through the microscope, dissecting bird pellets, or visiting aquariums or marine museum.

Most middle school science courses are an introduction to science-related disciplines, including a little the sciences of chemistry, physics, biology as well as earth science. Children can earn high school credits in science, too. If your child is involved in the high school level of science then you may include it in the transcript of high school.

Chapter 8: Teaching Other Middle School Topics

Social Studies

Social studies are an essential area of study that is taught each year. It may include subjects like the study of geography, history social, as well as recent events.

Make social studies fun. You don't need to include a text book unless you're planning to. Have fun making crafts, projects and eating food together with your child. Go to museums, or visit the field on excursions with your child. Children can also be taught through books, movies books, CDs Biographies, literature, and biographies. Make use of timelines, and even make some map.

In social studies, the aim is to create an understanding of the basics. When your child enters high school and is exposed to World War I, they will recognize that it happened just after George Washington in the timeline.

Foreign Language

Prior to beginning your study of foreign languages Begin with some basic supplementation to assist in making learning a new language simpler. It is important to learn Latin as well as Greek roots. The most effective way to master these roots is to play a game known as Rummy Roots. It's an enjoyable game as Go Fish. Your child will get more familiar with the meanings and implications of English suffixes and prefixes that originated from Latin as well as Greek. It's an excellent opportunity to let your child dip his foot into another languages.

Many homeschoolers begin with Latin as their initial foreign language. This can be beneficial because the majority of European languages have their roots in Latin. When you start learning Latin initially, you can help your child to master various languages. That's why that we began Latin at the middle of school, and after that, I started learning French while my kids were at high school. It was because the Latin studies made it simpler to master French.

When you're choosing a new language take into consideration that it's the easiest to learn one you're familiar with. Any amount of familiarity will help.

Language studies in foreign countries can involve writing, reading or speaking as well as listening to the spoken language. Learning about the geography and culture is also essential. Find out about the different countries and cultures in which the language is spoken. The study of the culture could make learning enjoyable. While I was at high school, we would make crepes during French class.

If your child follows the standard high school curriculum and you want to use it to earn the first credit for high school in a foreign language on your transcript.

Physical Education

P.E. could mean physical activity, or physical education or any combination of both. It could also include showing your child the importance that they take care your body. Exercise can be whatever your child is doing that causes sweat. The aim of P.E. is to be both fun and fitness. It teaches them that fitness can be fun since exercise can be fun.

Be aware that middle schoolers are subject to massive body transformations. Be sure to cover the health aspect during your P.E. class. I would recommend Total Health written by Susan Boe. The book was designed specifically for Christian schoolchildren around twenty years ago this book doesn't cover the unique issues that children today face. Whichever book you decide to read you choose, make sure to include the changing body of children and their health.

Be sure to also talk about the topic of purity and relationships. So, you'll be able to go to high school having had these vital discussions regarding the health of your body, sexual purity and the bonds between them.

It is also crucial to consider the basics of nutrition since your kids have been experiencing growth spurts. In these times of growth children often opt to eat as many junk food as they can. They need to be taught about nutrition, so that they do not depend on junk food for the sole source of energy. Learn good habits for them.

Experts agree to keep teens away from dieting. The word "diet" shouldn't be an option in the homes due to the issues in how kids view their body. Their body image can change at the time of preteens and teens.

It is important to restrict the use of technology to improve health. Children are more likely to engage in technology rather than playing on skateboards or the basketball. Limit the amount of the amount of technology you use in order to allow your child the opportunity to play out and play. Reduce your child's use of technology to allow their body to be able to develop in a normal way.

Focus on personal fitness and have enjoyable. Make sure you find a balance between having fun and safety. It's easy to become cautious and stop your child from leaving to play. However, youngsters must be taught that they can move around, and play for enjoyment.

Fine Art

Fine arts encompass theatre, music, art and dancing. It is possible to expose your child to any one (or greater if you are able to) of these fine art forms. Inspire personal expression through your child's creative development. The arts are hands-on subject matter, without examinations, or curriculum as well as playing whenever feasible.

The art field is not a strong one in my personal experience, and so I have used a curriculum. Other families have art as it is an integral part of the daily routine. The art of making isn't a subject that requires any difficulties in learning. Explore art with your child. It is your goal to stimulate naturally giftedness, exposing your child to the arts as well as music, theater and dance, to determine the one that they can be able to enjoy throughout their lives.

Choices

It is possible to include a variety of options for electives at middle school. Most often, Christian parents include a Bible class. As my kids attended middle school I were known as Cozy Couch Time. My boys and me listened to Josh McDowell's Youth

Devotions and discussed it. This was a fun gathering time for the whole family. There is a possibility of adding a bit of character education in addition. It is important to teach children what it takes to be a moral ethical person, with moral ethics, when they grow into adulthood.

The teaching of critical thinking is crucial. The books we used were our children's Building Thinking Skills collection of titles by Critical Thinking Co. They proved extremely beneficial in helping my kids develop their thinking abilities. When I first started the course, I didn't know that children could be taught spatial reasoning. I believed it was a skill you're born with or not.

Another option for electives that's usually offered at middle school, is the technological course. Be sure that your child is aware of the way computers function. It is equally important to use keyboards for your child to begin typing correctly. If they are going to the high school level, they must be able to write at a speed that is precise and fast.

Exam Training and Preparation

Testing skills are essential however, you should avoid testing too much. Make a simple annual test that will show the progress your child has made every year. They can stay away from future anxiety over tests as they're a element of daily life, similar to your annual trip for a visit to the physician. Each year's testing will show children that testing isn't frightening, they're just an aspect of everyday the daily routine.

Do not over-test in every discipline. Instead, concentrate on learning for the sake of learning and not on test practice.

Some parents contact me with concerns concerning taking the SAT or ACT exam. They understand that it is crucial to be able to get into college and would like to know if they need to prepare now at the middle of school. One of the best things you can do as a middle-schooler is to instruct your child to read mathematics, writing, and reading as well as teaching penmanship to ensure you are prepared for any examination.

Give your child the foundational knowledge that your child will be able to build upon to come back. It's not the right moment to prepare for tests This is the right moment to learn.

The boredom Busters to help Reluctant Kids

Create or find educational games. There are many games online that cover subjects. Make sure to incorporate hands-on learning wherever possible and aid in learning for your child. Your child will be able to learn more than what is written in the text, such as their meaning as well as a deeper understanding.

Chapter 9: In The Future High School And Beyond

Study and practice High School Record-Keeping

First step in keeping the correct homeschool records is to determine what lawful requirements are required. Read your state's law on homeschooling. After you've completed your research take care not to be worried about your state's school law because it's not the norm for homeschoolers. Find your state's homeschool laws here.

One mother contacted me as she was concerned over Ohio law governing the teaching of math. We did some research and came to the conclusion that Ohio homeschool law in the state said there was nothing specifically regarding math. Check out your state's homeschool laws be sure to not get confused with the laws governing public schools in the state. Be sure to know exactly the requirements for you both in the present and later on.

Once you've mastered the information needed, find out how to maintain the records of your high school and then practice keeping records. Record keeping at high school includes the creation of a transcript, course descriptions, and a list of readings. The goal of the middle grade is to know the three components of record keeping, so you don't have to be scared about high school. Learn more about recording your homeschool records in my book Set records. Records Straight.

Once you are learning about keeping records and implementing this, you should keep at a steady time for yourself and your style of learning. If you are learning at a rapid pace, you'll become stressed, exhausted out, and shattered by being a homeschooling teenager. Also, you don't want to be learning too much in a short time. If you do this, you'll fall behind, be scared or panicky, then eventually stop homeschooling in high school.

Plan your classes at high school. The plan could involve covering French as a foreign language, and getting a grasp of Latin at middle school, so that French can be taught at high school. Planning for your high school classes could help students to create a big image of the subjects you wish to learn in the near future.

Earn credits for early high school

If you're practicing making transcripts Be aware that some classes that your child took at middle school could be counted as early high school credits. Higher than Algebra 1 or higher, high school science, a complete grade of foreign languages using an academic program that is standard for high schools as well as the equivalent of a college or high school equivalent class may be counted as a total high school credits in your child's transcript.

You may be awarded one high school credit once you have completed your textbook or class. Then, you can include it in your child's cumulative grade-point average (GPA) on their academic transcript of the high school.

Research College Financing

It can be a bit confusing to figure out how to finance college It is important to explore possibilities early. In middle school, it's the right period to start thinking about colleges to ensure your child's success. Set up challenging classes for high school. This is a great option to afford the college of your choice. Your child will have an opportunity to be awarded merit scholarships as well as the most lucrative scholarship by arranging challenging courses. Mathematics, science, as well as foreign languages are crucial classes that will lead you towards scholarships.

In the event that your child receives merit scholarship, you should think about the cost of the college. Consider researching ways to apply for scholarships today as soon as your kids have reached middle school. You will then be well-informed about how to apply for scholarships before your child is in high school.

Even though earlier is more convenient but it's never enough time to save for your college. Find out more about the 529 plan for college. It is the most popular bargain currently, however there are also state investments plans that are similar to the 529. A lot of them enter use in middle school, and you must research the plans before your child is in the eighth grade. Discover the many strategies for investing and begin saving money right now. Consider the assistance you could be eligible for from colleges. Utilize FAFSA's FAFSA forecaster.

You could save a particular amount of your earnings, and put it in a savings account from the beginning. Each time you receive an increment, make sure you place the amount in the savings.

There is also the option of saving the amount you earn per week either per month or for the entire year. You might want to save the tax refund you receive or your cash for Christmas each year. It is also possible to save inheritances and gifts. You might want to ask your grandparents for funds to save for college instead of gift cards for your child to increase their college savings every birthday.

Find out about tax deductions and taxes that come with putting the money away to attend college. Examine whether tax deductions will aid in saving on tax every year.

There are loans available to finance college. Financial advisors generally adhere to the rule of one-third. The general rule is to not save more than one-third of what is expected to be the expenses of attending college. Other funds can be sourced from different sources.

Middle Schoolers in good health

Be sure that your kids are in good health. Instill healthy habits in them so that they can become healthy teenagers as well as adults. Your sleep needs will change once your children enter middle school. Be sure that they have the proper sleep they need, and get to bed at the right time, so that they get up at the right the right time.

The growth spurts of a child can have a profound impact on children's diet. Make sure your child is eating an appropriate diet during an increased growth rate. As my kids went through growth spurts they played sport simultaneously, which meant that our food cost went up significantly.

Be sure that your child is getting sufficient exercise in order to keep the physical condition of their body both now and into the coming years. Help them understand the importance of keeping limits. Inform them that using technology can drastically impact their physical fitness and their health. Make sure you touch on their health as there isn't a second chance to talk about the subject.

Make sure to keep in mind that the age of maturity varies. Being a registered nurse I have learned that medical emergencies could have the biggest impact on changes in maturity. If your child is affected by an illness that is major this can affect their mental maturity by two years.

If your child behaves like an eighth grader today, then breaks an ankle and winds in undergoing surgery, they could be as a fifth-grader for several weeks. If you suffer from a medical issue be prepared for your child to appear younger than what they typically do.

Chapter 10: Produce A Short Film

My absolute beloved Unit Studies we ever did was film-making. I enjoyed giving my kids a short prompt, and then seeing their responses with the actual film that either made me is awed or sad Sometimes both.

Although I thought that film making could stimulate their creativity, I didn't realize what it could do to their thinking sides. They discovered that they needed to design each shot and film with great care to tell their story in the way they wanted.

For this assignment, teenagers are required to write, film and edit their own short film. It can be anything from a single minute of silent film, to a more extensive production with actors, scripts, as well as scene adjustments. Every format is sure to entertain!

GUIDELINES

Create the idea of a film. This could be the toughest stage! If they're really stuck provide them with a area, prop, or the dialogue line and let them go from there. the moment.

Draw a storyboard of the action.

Create a production schedule. The production schedule should comprise all of the following steps and deadline dates.

Create an outline. Even if it's simply a single minute silent film, you could create a script for the action and feelings being depicted. Find "how to create an script" for a better understanding of the elements of a script include!

Make sure you have costumes, props and props.

Cast members. Collaboration with a person different from a child will add some professionality to your project!

Encourage your child to master proper camera skills. While teenagers can definitely make films using their intuition There are a few established and tried-and-true methods of making a film that conveys specific moods and feelings. There's plenty of YouTube videos to watch and also films that are short and online. I have a fun Film Making Unit Study available at https://www.teacherspayteachers.com/Store/Elyse-Hudacsko.

Make the film.

Edit the movie. There are a lot of edit apps for free. We love WeVideo.

Add sound effects and music.

Make an Animatronic

Each year, for Halloween, the friends we have come up with a thrilling haunted house within their backyard. It's full of scary animatronics. They have enthralled my children since my daughters were young.

The other year, we decided to give it a go creating our own. The result was an angry cat who wiggled its tail, and then an abrasive hand which was able to rotate over the grass. It's not the most terrifying of Halloween decorations, however it was extremely fun to make our custom.

Through this activity, teenagers create and design an animatronic. (For Halloween, or any other reason they think of!) This task requires some basic motors, at least the basic animatronic and even more enthusiastic teens could investigate more sophisticated electronics.

GUIDELINES

Discuss the budget.

It is important to understand the basic principles for making a moveable decorative. "Make" provides a wonderful outline of 4 easy and affordable animatronics. https://makezine.com/2017/10/25/4-animated-halloween-decorations-you-can-build-on-budget/ . Teens also have the option of becoming better at sexiness if they choose!

Design a decoration. The designers will have to create both the interior structure and the exterior decoration.

Make a list of materials.

Find the materials you need in stores or online.

Create the animatronic design. Teenagers might need assistance using electric tools!

Add decorative elements of your animatronic.

Code a Video Game

A few days ago, my daughter stared at me and told me, "I want to code for a online game." I sat in a blank stare. I was unsure of how to start and was terrified attempt to introduce the art of programming to my 13-year young.

And I decided to do what every amazing homeschool mothers do. I searched it on Google. I found an excellent software from MIT to help first-time programmers. My daughter learned the basics of programming with the program for free and created several games everyone enjoyed playing. My daughter, for one, decided that she preferred playing games on video instead of writing them but she did gain an understanding of the process by which software is created.

Teens create a game using code. The great thing about this project is that it's simple (think Pong) or a more complex one (like Minecraft) depending on the level of skill as well as their interest.

GUIDELINES

Download the programming program. If you are a beginner in programming I strongly suggest Scratch which is available from MIT. It's free and comfortable. You can definitely look into other options, and experienced developers can make use of the tools they have already mastered.

Find out how to code. If your teenager doesn't have the skills to code buy them a book! If they opt to use Scratch to get started, they can find excellent books such as "Scratch Programming for Teens" written by Jerry Lee Ford, Jr. which will help students learn the fundamentals.

Create an idea for an idea of a game that they want to develop. The newer developers will prefer to make things easy to start their game!

Create the components of the game.

1. Main Characters - Who is this person? what are they like? What powers do they possess?

2. Location - where are the games taking place?

3. What is the main character attempting to accomplish?

4. The Villains/Challenges: Who or What will stop the main character from attaining their objective? How do they appear? What are their powers?

5. Levels - What are the various scenarios that the character must traverse?

6. Scoring: How does the game be scored? Are they bonus points? do they have points, or is it just winnings?

The game is described as a storyboard. Through the creation of a photo with a description for each phase in the game the information that needs to be programmed is much more apparent. Help your child list every single thing which are expected to take place. More details you can provide, the more detailed!

Chapter 11: Design The Fairy Trail

As my children were young and awed by fairytales. This meant that I was also fascinated by fairies, and was always searching to find a fairy tale or dress-up doll. A few days ago, I discovered the mom load. A fairy-tale trail.

My two tiny fairies on the forest trails and then we walked. A few minutes later, one of the girls saw an adorable house constructed of stones, moss and twigs. A perfect house to be one of the fairytale characters. Each few yards was another beautiful home. Every one of them was constructed from organic material. A few were small lean-tos, with the occasional stick stool for the fairy to rest on while others were lavish homes featuring dining and lounges, hammocks and even feather beds!

In the years that followed, we attempted to build our the fairy homes of our own and hide the houses along local trails with the intention of delighting the other fans of fairy tales! Our minds were pushed by turning twigs and branches and leaves into common things and architectural marvels.

Through this activity, teenagers will create a fairy trail. In addition to getting to test their planning, making and building skills but they'll have the chance to bring a bit of magic to local children. It's so much enjoyable that I would like the project to be a family affair or a social event!

GUIDELINES

Choose which natural trail in the area you want to transform into a fairy-tale trail. Since the homes comprise of only organic materials, I would not worry about putting the structures along a trail however you could ask the owner of the trail for permission.

Decide whether the project is a group or solo project. Your teenager can be responsible for the entire designing and construction themselves, or delegate this project with the help of members of the family or with colleagues. Making the hike together can add some additional planning abilities for your project!

Create a calendar. It must include the the time needed to plan, collect the materials, construct, and then place the structures. If the building project is involving other people, there should be discussions and communications in the program.

Design homes and household objects. There are many excellent books such as "Fairy Houses The Art of Creating Fantasy Houses that appeal to Fairy Folk" by Sally Smith with plans.

Collect ingredients. Also, the tools required for building using.

Create fairy houses.

Hike out to find the houses along the trails.

Continue to make progress! Although our first project was finished, we were thrilled to building new homes every occasionally to make it easier to follow the trail. We hoped other people would enjoy it too!

Take Over the Kitchen

The greatest college graduation gift I got was cooking classes. 8 classes taught me how to chop, sauté, and bake. Also, I learned how to make souffle! However, even more crucial than the technical expertise was the discussion the teacher was having with us about food preparation.

The students learned how to look up recipes and then use this information to make a list of items as well as a plan. We discussed the importance of making healthy, delicious dishes that would meet the requirements of guests or families. We were able to keep an eye on the budget while making a decision on what to eat. We gained the ability to not just cook, but also how to design the menu.

Through this activity, students are expected to create a nutritious and tasty menu program for the entire week. Though this task is certainly difficult, the kids enjoy it since the outcomes are real (they are able to enjoy them!) And they're being shown the responsibility and control over the family that they don't usually have. Some may ask them to complete this task again!

GUIDELINES

Choose the order of your meals during the entire week. My teens receive an agenda with take-out on Fridays as well as the meals that we require throughout the week. My calendar includes lunch, however breakfast is not included.

Talk about the meaning of "healthy" or "delicious" refers to for your family. At my home, we eat lunch with salad every day as well as at least one veggie and sometimes we eat dessert at least once during the week.

Talk about any diet restrictions. There's a vegetarian in our family as well as one who has a extremely low-carb and, while we offer a single meal to our family members, we ensure that we have choices for everyone.

Discussion of the budget. This adds a new level of difficulty to the task but it's essential when you have a daily food budget. It is a good concept to guide teens to make decisions and come up with compromises.

Create your own meal plan. An easy grid that has the dates of the week at the top, and meal times on the sides works great. I've asked my children to utilize a spreadsheet application (for additional skill development) but paper does the job well.

Explore websites and cookbooks to find recipes.

Make a list of your shopping. I ensure that my teenagers are aware of the layout and design of the supermarket in order to make their lists more organized.

You can send your teen to the store for shopping. Teens may shop alone or, if have just started shopping at the department, join parents to help with any concerns.

Prepare, cook, and Serve. I prefer to be present in another room when my son cooks a delicious dish in case they ask doubts or come across some new method that isn't available on YouTube!

"Bon Appetit!

Make Stop Motion Animation Stop Motion Animation

My daughter and I attended a short online course with each other to make simple stop-motion animations. This made up part of my "Lunchtime Creativity" series I designed to aid my single daughter conquer her block in the art world.

Although I was hoping that it could be the chance to have a relaxing, non-pressured 15-minute art challenge over a period of time, it ended up being something we enjoyed and put lots of work into. Our short, quick animations took on a new life that was their own and became into excellent mini-movies.

For this assignment, teenagers are required to create a stop-motion animation. As they create a story plan as well as complete the technical requirements as well, the task also lets the imagination run wild. It's so straightforward that it can be completed at the at the kitchen table.

GUIDELINES

Create the idea of a film. This is the most difficult stage! If you are stuck, Give them a persona or a place, as well as some emotional response.

Storyboard the story. Animations using stop motion can be very simple and quick however, you should encourage your teenager to make at minimum six distinct scenes within the film to take us from beginning to to ending.

You can choose between drawing an animation by using collage pieces. The process is the same. Drawing, your teenager will draw every frame by changing the positioning and appearance of the characters. When creating collages, your child is creating parts of a characters from pieces of paper. They'll alter the pieces to modify the appearance and pose of the person. They can also do the two with possibly drawing the background, as a collage and then the person drawn.

Install Stop Motion on their smartphone. We love Stop Motion Studio

Create the film rig. The easiest method to do this is to use a couple of large books as well as a bit of clear plexiglass. The teen should place the books on top of each other until they're about six to eight inches tall Then, place the plexiglass onto and hang it on the edge of the pile. Add another book over the top, to keep the plexiglass in place. The filmers will place their smartphone in the plexiglass, and placing the animation or collage pieces under, and then take a photo using the app every time they alter their location.

Sound effects, and music.

Begin a Business

In my teen years, I had always thought of an idea to start a company. However, my parents snatched my ideas and made into realities. It was a fact is that I was only as a child and was unable to ever start a business.

If my daughters approached me with ideas for business I support the idea completely. It is my belief that the business they have created won't grow. Isn't it the same for many adult companies? Instead of being focused on the whether or not I succeed my focus is on learning amazing life skills, such as communications and marketing.

Through this program, teenagers are expected to start their own enterprise. Every business can be successful the job, but one they enjoy will be able to have more success and will be a lot more enjoyable! (And make sure you don't try to squash their ideas. It is likely that no one will have a frenzied search for their lipsticks or their parakeet watch service but nobody is certain!)

GUIDELINES

Come up with an idea for a business.

Discuss what that they'll require into the business.

1. An idea for a product or service

2. An elevator pitch

3. An item or service that has been evaluated

4. Price and cost details

5. Budgets for starting up

6. Packaging and labels (if required)

7. Stores and websites that sell their products or services.

8. A plan for marketing

9. Marketing material

Write an outline of your business that includes each of the above items. Teenagers can locate examples online, or they can make their own.

Examine the plan of business with an consultant.

Locate the capital needed to start.

Fill in the details of the plan of business. It could be a great idea to schedule a regular meeting of status with your child to determine what they're doing and to determine if they require any assistance from an adult.

Sell and produce.

Create an Act

Who hasn't thought of putting the pieces together for a show in their youth? or at the very least, seeing Jo, Meg, Beth as well as Amy perform it as in "Little women"? The act of putting on a show is a common ritual of adolescence!

Teens create a production. It will not only stretch their creative brains, but it also will require a tremendous amount of coordination as well as more importantly, negotiations. It may be a huge gathering or simply an intimate family-only event!

GUIDELINES

Look for an original script. Short scripts are ideal, and could even be some scenes from an extended performance. A longer script can be a great option for those who are looking to take on the task and compose their own script in the event that they want.

Choose a time and the venue. Make sure that teens allow themselves sufficient time to prepare and that the date is not in conflict with something other vital.

Auditions and casting the actors. It's important to be aware of every actor's availability to perform during the show and rehearsals, so make sure you ask!

Create a rehearsal schedule.

Provide the actors with the schedule for rehearsals and script.

Conduct rehearsals. Just prior to the show, there'll be an dress rehearsal.

Chapter 12: Take A Trip

My very first plan-of-the-month project was back in the third grade. I arranged a family trip in Washington DC. The time was before advent of internet technology and I still remember visiting the library to look through books on travel and to find destinations' addresses from phone books, so that I could make a list of brochures! I scoured our activities we planned to accomplish, and scheduled for them within the duration of our vacation and then wrote down reservations and tickets.

Even to this day, I recall how proud of myself for having planned such a memorable trip (including seeing the White House) for my family. My skills in planning trips learned in my early years are still useful to me throughout my travels around all over the globe in my later years.

For this assignment, teenagers can plan their own family vacation. Planning a major vacation can be an overwhelming task, however organizing a trip for just a day provides teenagers with an opportunity to develop their planning skills. There is no limit to the location, just take off!

GUIDELINES

Pick the destination along with the date, time, and budget for your itinerary. The trip which is within one place is the most convenient but don't hesitate to take them on an extended trip.

Discuss with everyone in the family on the things you would like them to participate in. Planning a trip all the family members will love begins with knowing the priorities of every family member (great dining options, no trekking!) as well as being crystal clear about the absolute things to do (see The Taj Mahal!) and no-no's (taking an air balloon ride).

Discuss any travel or time limitations. The eager planners might be too excited about all the tasks to accomplish that they fail to figure out what time they will take and how long travel will take between them.

Make a document of planning for your excursion. My teens are encouraged to utilize a spreadsheet application (to improve their tech abilities) however, paper is just well. It should have dates that run down the sides as well as the top items such as the location of the day, arrangements for sleeping and dining choices, activities to do, expenses as well as travel time. There should be a space with notes, too.

Find out what you can do such as sleeping arrangements, eating options at all places you're planning to visit and include them on their itinerary documents. Website links are required together with the hours and open days. It is also important to note the cost and the travel time between different places and activities.

Reread the plan.

Talk about any concerns, and make changes to the plan. Continue to revise until the plan is working!

Make reservations. It's usually an excellent idea to be alongside your child as they create the reservation. At the very least, agree that you will examine the reservation prior to when they click "confirm".

Bon voyage!

Decorate a Cake

My previous job I ran a bakeshop and designed absurd cakes that resembled like real seagulls and hamburgers as well as caps for men. My kids were always excited to see the show, and as they were older, I would help.

In the past, they had a desire to learn more about the art of cake decorating. They completed the task of making, designing, and baking as well as decorating cakes. It was a great (and tasty) project gave them the incentive to not just be inventive and imaginative, but also organised and determined.

For this activity, teenagers can design, bake, and decorate cakes. You can bake one for special occasions or just for enjoyable to enjoy a delicious cake at any time of the evening.'

GUIDELINES

Choose the design that the cake will be. Cakes are typically cake with tiered sides (like on the wedding) decorated at the top and sides, or they could be made (think Ace of Cakes) in order to resemble everyday things.

Design a cake. Ask your child to pick up an ebook such as Debbie Brown's "Magical Cakes", Colette Peters "The Art of Cake Decorating" and Toba Garrett's "Professional Cake Decorating" for some inspiration. Although they may want to decorate their cake different (different shades, flowers or other decorations) It is helpful to have a standard guideline to follow therefore I wouldn't recommend making a unique layout.

Make a plan. Following the recipe of the cake they have chosen Your teen should create plans for when the tasks have to be done in accordance with when they would like their cake to be completed. The shopping needs to be completed. There are some decorations that can be planned ahead. Cakes should cool off after baking and then rest when they are iced. Reading the instructions thoroughly is essential!

Shop. Your teenager is likely to be able locate the majority of cake ingredients as well as the icing at your local shop, however certain decorating supplies and other tools may have to be purchased from the craft store or on line. NY Cake is my favorite shop, both in-person and on the internet!

Bake the cake. Then prepare the filling and the icing.

Make decorations. If the directions from the books they are following aren't enough There are lots of cakes decorating techniques available on YouTube.

Make the cake.

Designate your cake.

Create the Magic Show

Every year, we have the most glamorous Halloween celebration featuring amazing costumes, an amazing DJ and tasty food. But the one thing that draws me every time is the entertainment. I could be there for hours, watching him perform in complete amazement and competition.

It is not just about learning the art of the art of magic and creating shows an excellent way to develop your skill It is an important abilities that make people look good after a while when they attend dinner parties and other corporate celebrations!

Through this program, teenagers are taught how to perform magic. They will then design the show for their loved ones, or even for the entire town!

GUIDELINES

Learn to do magic. We are awestruck by "Penn and Teller teaches the art of magic" accessible through Masterclass. They can find books or videos about magic tricks.

Create a magician. Teens should incorporate tricks they've mastered, and then write down what they'll be saying to please people in the middle. Naturally, they'll require a great costume, or a fantastic support person!

Practice. Doing it with one of your friends or family member will allow your teenager to master their routine, and also work on the tension.

Plan an event. The performance will be advertised and scheduled.

Astonish and amaze your audience!

Sew an Costume

There's no doubt that I've always longed for an unpackaged Halloween costume. However, I would always get one that my father made. (That was way more attractive than what any of my peers were wearing.)

Naturally, I took my dad's passion for creating costumes from scratch and I was able to do the same with my girls, too. They also got the bug, and after they reached a certain age, began creating their own. Every year, it's been a wonderful opportunity to practice creating a costume and follow the directions along with getting into sewing!

For this activity, teenagers can sew costumes for Halloween, or a cosplay costumes. They will require an sewing machine to complete this project, but they're cheap to acquire, or they can be rented out or borrowed.

GUIDELINES

Visit the store for fabric and pick an appropriate pattern from a book. Many pattern books come with the section for costumes, as well as book that specialize in costumes.

You should read the reverse of the pattern in order to comprehend what materials are required to complete the sewing project. If your teenager is brand not a pro at sewing, staff at the fabric stores will be of great help in determining the materials they require.

Purchase the necessary materials. Make sure you have thread! Also, a pair of scissors for sewing and pins.

Chapter 13: Organize A Dinner Party

There's something enchanting about an evening celebration. It could be transform your small dining area into a five-star restaurant.

Making a great dinner celebration requires the creativeness of an artist, and the expertise of an experienced Marine. This is what creates the magic!

For this assignment, teenagers are expected to plan and organize an event for dinner. The event could be a surprise an event for their family or friends or yours. It's hard to say what is more relaxing But preparing well can make your evening much more enjoyable!

GUIDELINES

Choose who is at the dinner gathering. If your teenager isn't used to the idea select family members or acquaintances who will not be upset the event if it doesn't go according to plan.

Set a time and theme to the event. The date should not be too far from anything or anything else is essential. The theme could be the season, or a particular style of cuisine, or an event that is fun and funny.

Discuss any limitations regarding the celebration. It is possible that there are some foods that require special preparation or are allergic to.

Create a menu. It is suggested to have some appetizers when guests arrive, then the soup or salad courses along with an entree or dessert. It's a great idea to bring only a couple of dishes that require immediate care.

Set the table for your event. Utilizing the tablecloths, dishes and napkins that you own is a great option. However, your teenager can personalize your table using candles, a centerpiece as well as a couple of other ornamental things.

Create a calendar. Teenagers must plan the tasks they need to complete ahead of time as well as some tasks for the day. These tasks that have been scheduled are able to be scheduled at the end of each day, while any last minute projects should be planned right to the minute so that everything can run efficiently.

Check out the menu. The guidance of an experienced cook will help to ensure that the time is effective.

Note down a shopping list.

Shop.

Set up the table, and cook the food.

Serve and clean. You could also offer to wash the dishes for your child at the end of the night!

Decorate the Room

Each summer over the last five years, either one (or both) of my kids desired to revamp their bedroom. However, after a major change between them, between "little girl" to "teen" I decided that I didn't feel up for the job.

Then I let them take on the work. Armed with only a tiny budget, and plenty of flexibility, they completed their renovation projects with the same ease as seasoned HGTV hosts! They understood they could not count on me be pushing to get this project completed and that when they needed something different, they would need to work and follow through with the plan.

The teens are expected to redecorate their room. It's likely to be on their own! This can be a major undertaking however a teenager can and do this independently. I promise!

GUIDELINES

Discuss your budget. It ranges from $1000 for a small refresh up or a complete brand new space.

Discuss any restrictions. It could be that painting is not an option. Maybe an heirloom dresser can't be touched. The walls may have holes that not be allowed. It is important to make the restrictions clear!

Create a scale plan. Teens can create it with a pen or paper, or by using an app such as "Plan Your Home" as well as "Room Sketcher". You will have to determine the dimensions of their space as well as their current furniture before getting it set out.

Create their own room. Based on their scale it is possible to rearrange or change furniture, and take notes on color changes as well as accessories changes.

Make a vision boards. Print out for your teenager their new purchases together with the size plans, color swatches and the plan and then place the images on a poster board. The prices of the new products should be listed too.

Discuss the concept. Before work is completed, the teen must show their vision boards. This is when you can vote, propose, and even congratulate!

Create a calendar. Everyone doesn't want a lengthy remodeling project, therefore teens must decide what needs to be completed, and in which sequence.

You can shop or buy new products through the web. Remember to stay within your budget!

Paint or assembly, and decorate.

Create an Gingerbread House

Each year, I construct an gingerbread home. I've created copies of my house as well as of my favorite, the Pyramids of Giza. I've built beach houses as well as the Eiffel Tower. There was once an Lenni Lenape longhouse. Every year, my girls have been a blessing.

When they built gingerbread homes together, they were able to bake and decorate. They also learnt to master the math and measurements required to construct the houses, and they've explored different designs for architecture and developed into competent problem solvers as making a home from cake can be an enormous error that's which is just waiting to happen!

Teens are building a gingerbread home. Alongside the necessary planning skills to move from an empty bowl of flour, molasses and even a little Molasses into a work of art they'll gain some resilience and perseverance! This one creates chaos, so prepare. It is my guarantee that the end result will be something special!

GUIDELINES

Pick a house design. It is highly recommended to purchase an ebook such as "The Gingerbread architect" from Susan Matheson or "The Gingerbread Book" by Allen Bragdon that has ready drawn plans, even if your child is highly skilled in math or has architectural capabilities.

Make a list of what you need to buy. While they will require the ingredients for icing and gingerbread, but there may be some essential equipment and decorating materials. It is essential to go through the directions to learn what they will need.

Create a paper-based template. Even if your child uses a template in an article, they'll require a complete size template using sheet of paper.

Bake the gingerbread slices.

Prepare the icing.

Create the house. Make sure your child knows that this is the place where a bit of problem solving could be needed! The pieces of your house connect completely. It is necessary to employ support structures (like soup cans) or perhaps a third pair of hands, or perhaps pins. Then they'll have wait until the items dry, and possibly revise their plan for decoration in order in order to disguise some troublesome places.

Create a home decoration. Your teen may decorate their home exactly like the guidelines by the guide, they may unleash their imagination with a variety of changes to make it their own.

Make an Intentional Garden

When I was a teenager I can remember the first carrot I ever grew. I remember plucked it out of the ground, then brushing the dirt away and devouring it until I could eat the leaves straight from the garden. It's true that the carrot is pretty much all I've grown that I have ever had the pleasure of growing however I've always tried.

My garden may consist of mostly simple-to-manage herbs as well as a few cherry tomatoes in a pot, allowing my kids to get involved in cultivating their own vegetables is crucial for me. Even if it's only enough to create a little salad!

Teens are constructing a garden to start. An entire outdoor space or a couple of windowsill pots for a start is a great option for a garden!

GUIDELINES

Discuss where the garden is going to be.

Research the best plants to cultivate. Your teenager will have to know what every plant requires in terms of sunlight and space, and make certain they've got it within their gardens.

Learn the basics of how to plant and care for every thing in the garden. "Gardening for Dummies" is an excellent place to begin.

Buy seeds or plants. The price is greater to buy plants, but it could be easier for the new gardener.

Buy any soil fertiliser, food or other fertilizer required.

Plant your gardens. Teenagers need to be aware that seed planting usually takes place indoors during the first days of spring, so they need to be prepared for it!

Go to the garden.

Enjoy and harvest!

Cook the entire Cookbook

Have you seen the film "Julie and Julia"? The film told the tale of author Julie Powell who decided to cook all the recipes from Julia Child's "Mastering the art of French cooking" and then write a blog about the process. I've always been fascinated by Julie's adventure, but was simply a bit jealous that she came up with an amazing concept! In the end, I stole her concept and began cooking by reading the Thomas Keller books!

I not only stepped up my cooking skills and improve my cooking skills, I also learned how to tackle some tough circumstances that I'd rather not have faced. For instance, Julie who had take on the task of making a recipe that required she removed the bones of the duck. It was my experience that sometimes it is necessary to overcome obstacles must be negotiated through to get to the goal. In the end they will result in slight discomfort but no major injury!

Through this program, teenagers can cook through the pages of the entire book. The participants will not only gain the ability to cook, but also an immense sense of achievement. It's a huge one but can be controlled by the volume and the complexity of the recipe and also the deadline for finalization. Think of all the incredible foods you'll enjoy!

GUIDELINES

Choose an appropriate cookbook. The comfort of your teen with cooking and passion about this endeavor will lead them in making a wise selection. Selecting a book that is too big and complex isn't the best recipe to be successful.

Discuss the timeline. Do they cook every day, and then wrap it up over the course of a month? Perhaps cook once every week for all year to cook?

Create a timetable of times they'll work on each dish.

You could consider the idea of creating a blog, Vlog, or an Instagram account for tracking your progress. In some cases, being accountable to your followers can give you the motivation to push through certain stumbling blocks.

Chapter 14: Put Your Money Into The Stock Market

While I was in my senior year of high school as a part of math class, we were each pretending to make investments on the stock market. The students were provided with a sum that was "money" and were able to choose the stocks we would like to be investing in. After that, we tracked their performance throughout the day before deciding if we wanted to invest or sell. We were all so excited that it seemed like we had forgotten that it wasn't real money!

The same thing happened using my homeschooled teenagers. They were given actual money to invest. A bank account can be opened for your child with as little as $500.

Teens can invest their money into the stock market. This isn't just an excellent idea but also it is also a good investment for the future of their finances.

GUIDELINES

Discussion of the stock market. Briefly explain to them of how it functions.

Open an account with a brokerage. The eTrade platform is a good choice. You can even buy items through the stock account of yours. Or you can set up a faux account!

Decide on how much you want to put into. It could be money that you donate to them, any the savings they've got or fake money.

Find out more about investing. There are many amazing books such as "Investing for Beginners" written by Eric Tyson, "Buffettology" by Mary Buffett, and "Teenvestor" written by Emmanuel Modo.

Purchase stocks.

Every once periodically on stocks, and then make a decision about purchasing new shares or selling a few. They can decide for themselves. This is the best way to gain knowledge.

Create an Historical Cookbook

When we are studying the past, my children insist that we cook a meal during that time almost all the time.

It is a lot of fun when you try recipes created long back. Understanding the various ingredients, recipes and eating styles of the past is an excellent opportunity to discover about old civilizations and the ancestors of our own.

For this assignment, teenagers are expected to create a cookbook with recipes from the past. The students can decide to write about all aspects of the past, or just the story of a specific area or country or even a specific date.

GUIDELINES

Select a specific location, and/or time frame.

Locate recipes using their place of origin and date.

Research unique materials, techniques, or ingredients with additional studies.

Rewrite every recipe by explaining the ingredients, methods and equipment and the substitutions that we could make in the present. It's one thing to take a recipe and add it in your book, but a different aspect is to really understand the recipe and instruct other cooks to follow the recipe.

Prepare the recipes, and snap photos. Teenagers may take photos of the end product, possibly certain ingredients or perhaps a small portion aspects of the recipe.

Make the form of a book. Teens may create a book or start blogs with the recipes, so other people are able to find and utilize the recipes.

Include a bit of background or a story prior to sharing the recipe. The ability to give the reader an idea of when the dish may be served and how it came to be can add a great deal of value.

Start a Teen Magazine

Some time ago, someone I know shared with me the way her son began a magazine. This was the first thing I added on the items I'd like to provide my kids with an opportunity to participate in!

The magazine that my friend's daughter founded was devoted to art and features work from local teenagers and poets, writers as well as comics, photographers and much more. It's published quarterly online and is a fantastic meeting place for teens in the area.

Teens will create magazines for teens specifically for teens.

GUIDELINES

Come up with ideas for magazines. Fashion, art, science and religion. Whatever you are obsessed with.

Choose if they're likely to be the head of the publication, or form a team to oversee the magazine.

Find out the details of the publication. It will be printed or digital? (Blurb is an excellent site to create papers magazines.) What is the frequency at which it will be released? What kinds of articles will appear in the magazine? What is the title?

Make contact with family members, friends and members of the public to request submissions. Please include the deadline!

Create a template to be used in the magazine. Lucidpress is a fantastic option for preparing magazines. It can also be created with Google Docs or even as web-based.

Lay out the magazine, including all the entries.

The magazine should be published and let people know about it! Make sure that readers are aware of the process to send their submissions in the following issue!

Create the publication of a Children's Book

As a young person, I was writing a wonderful kids' book called "Lizzie The Ladybug" which is located in the local elementary school library that kids can check to read and take pleasure in.

Teens are expected to write and illustrate a book for children. Making a children's book can be an excellent opportunity for teenagers to stretch their creativity and have fun doing it.

GUIDELINES

Create ideas for a book. Teenagers need to be able to identify two characters, an intro, a storyline, a conflict as well as a conclusion.

Note down the tale. Be aware that most children's books only include a few words on the page!

Draw illustrations for the text. The artists will be enthralled by making their own drawings. Others teens could ask an illustration partner or create their own artwork using sticks, collages photos, or any other thing that can provide visual appeal.

Have someone proofread and edit your work.

Publish your book. Teens can publish their book on Kindle Direct Publishing for free! They can also purchase discount copies for local shops to market.

Organize an Charity Scavenger Hunt

My daughter and I took part in this incredible world-wide scavenger hunt. We joined with other teams that came from around the globe on the internet and had a blast creating portraits from rubbish, attending unflattering sweater discussions, and feeding one another with a 6 foot spoon and much more.

We had a wonderful experience that we figured this would be an excellent concept for the local neighborhood. In addition, if the children could plan it the project would be an awesome idea.

Teens can design and plan an scavenger hunt. They will not only need to think of concepts, but they'll also have control the hunt in the manner of an enterprise to ensure that it goes smoothly.

GUIDELINES

Determine the logistics to conduct the hunt. It is necessary to plan a time, the exact location as well as how teams are made, how signups take place, how the list will be distributed, and how this hunt is evaluated. What will winners will receive. be tempted to organize the hunt for an annual fundraiser for charity, and then make a charge the participants.

Contact the town in the event that you believe approval may be required.

Create a ad to advertise the hunting. The flyers could be placed in the town, emails may be sent out, and post on social media could be created.

Manage sign ups. You may need to utilize an app for sign-ups such as the Sign Up Genius or just take the sign ups through email.

Make rules to ensure everyone is secure.

Note down items for the scavenger hunt.

Create instructions that let hunters know the best way to send things.

Note: Send reminders to all those who signed up just a few days prior to.

Get started on your search.

Note the scores and announce the winning submission!

Chapter 15: The Year That Changed Everything

March 2020. The Covid-19 virus was a hammer. Nearly every child around the globe was at home schooled. Parents took on the roles of educators. Imagine! The question was never even asked for to be asked, they were just handed into.

It's true that the Covid-19 altered almost everything. Parents were equally terrified and confused like their kids. Post-Covid, we live in an entirely different place. The way we think, feel and behave differently. Now more than ever, we must examine what we do and the reasons behind it. What is more crucial than our kids? Work is necessary. Do you have the ability to perform both in addition to all the other tasks that must be completed every day? Sure, you won't need to be educating your child for six hours every day, don't you think?

But, who said you have to work 6 hours every day? What if I informed you that if you were a homeschooler you could take shorter time?

"But I've been away for a while since I attended the school. Are I smart enough? Did you know that math in fifth grade was extremely difficult? What do you do to solve mixed fractions? It seems like I'm not educated enough to tutor an high school student. How much will this be going cost us? There isn't a great computer. Do you know of any support groups to help with this?"

Many questions and issues. We're here to inform that things don't need to be flawless. No matter what the motivation behind you to attempt to home school your kids You can try it when you'd like to.

Perhaps you're unsure of the concept of what educating your child in a home setting actually signifies. This is a good news flash for you covid-forced homeschooling isn't the essence of home-schooling. The term "home-schooling" can mean in general, but it's not an individual child seated at an electronic screen, in tears, for six hours per day, trying to figure out how to use Zoom as well as answering the questions displayed on the screen. This isn't educational or any learning. This is a shambles for parents and children.

Many children in 2020 did not receive proper instruction. A lot of teens did not receive the proper diploma. A lot of them fell behind and quit. They lost their friends, and were depressed and lonely.

On the other hand those with learning difficulties preferred being at home as the school day was never easy for them. Some kids were relieved from bullying at first in longer period of time.

A lot of parents stepped up the challenge and instructed their children using resources they could find, and soon realized that they could educate their teens and children--not simply because they earned a college degree or a degree, but simply because they were committed to helping their children comprehend. Doesn't that exactly what a teacher is?

There were parents who didn't have alarms were ringing at 6 a.m. and telling them to wake up, give their child an earful breakfast of cereal that was cold and put a lunch for the kids together. It was not a rush to drive the kids to school, nor having their children catch a bus or stroll in the morning chill. A lot of parents and their children had to reconsider their daily schedules and experience a more leisurely life.

What do you think of this lead you?

Do you appreciate the independence that homeschooling provides your entire family, but you aren't sure what to do? If yes, these chapters can help you make the right choice.

Chapter 16: Does It Make Sense To Home School My Children?

It's legal school your child at home throughout the 50 states in the United States. The trend is growing in popularity internationally too. Every state has its individual laws, and some prefer the concept of a home-schooling program over other states. Find the laws on homeschooling for your particular state, and then start from there.

Do I require an approved teacher in order to teach at home my kids?

No, it's not. It is true that many states will require parents to possess a high school degree or equivalent, when you don't have one, you are still able to teach your child. If that's the scenario, you'll require an assessor certified by the state who holds at least a bachelor's qualification. They will serve as your advocate. They are able to assist you with your concerns as well as suggest sources. These are people who have faith in the advantages of homeschooling, and more likely taught their children at home in the years following.

They leave the system of education themselves. The school pays to assess your child's work which is why they are working on your behalf you'll have the document of an official teacher stating that they've examined your child's academic work and the student's progress in academics corresponds to their abilities. The language you use gives both you and your child to have the flexibility to operate at your personal ability and pace.

This type of assessor through Facebook. Input the state's name into the Facebook search box, followed by "home-school group" (for instance, "Florida home-school group") Click to join. You can ask questions about the local assessor's name and someone else will be aware. Assessors are able to create magical ways to support and respect what you are doing within your school at home.

The majority of states require that you inform the local school district that you plan to homeschool your children. You can do this by submitting the Notice of Intent (Notice Of Intent) to the Home-school. Most states also require an end-of-the-school-year report. It could be an assessment based on standardized tests or a portfolio assessment conducted by a qualified teacher who administers the test like the one mentioned earlier. The assessor is employed by us and we don't conduct any standard test. The company pays a tiny annual cost to have Ben's work evaluated.

There are many methods that an examiner can look at the work of your child. It is possible to meet with them in person. However, during Covid the entire process was conducted on the internet, and some began having meetings using Zoom. The assessor of Ben's work is able to evaluate his work on a private, restricted Facebook page she was asked to join. I share photos on the page of his work all through the entire year. You are able to display the photos as little or as you like. You may get suggestions about what to focus on, but generally they believe that your student is performing at their best capabilities. It is then your responsibility to submit the assessed paperwork signed by the assessor along together with the NOI at start of the school year.

What exactly is home-schooling And Should We Utilize an Education Program?

Believe it or it's not true that there's nothing "exactly." It is your choice the option of choosing what to impart to your child, and the time, method you will be taught about it. It is also possible to select the day of the week that you would like to instruct and the length of time you'll spend with the subject you choose to cover every day. It is a vastly different process from public schools in the method of making it happen. You can accomplish the exact same amount of work school at home in three hours as the public school class could accomplish in six hours. It's not a long commute or changing class, and since the teacher-student ratio is higher, educating students one-on-one concepts and learning go much faster. This is a great benchmark for you to follow if think you require one.

1. Kindergarten Hour split into three

20-minute learning/playing/reading sections

1st - 2nd grade: 1 hour 30 minutes broken up

in three 30-minute playingor reading sections

3rd-4th grades 3 hours divided into three one-hour segments

5th to 6th grade 3- 4 hours split into three-to-four one-hour segments

7th-8th grades duration: 3-4 hours. sessions can run longer than the two-hour timeframe (we usually do 2 minutes in the early morning, and 2 hours during the afternoon and that gives plenty of time for different things! Big smile)

High School: as much as you can depending on tolerance

This is the normal "day at home school" will look as:

Routine for the morning: We like the fact that we do not have to awake to alarms. When we are awake, Ben takes care of his duties for the day that include cleaning up and making his bed, drinking water, taking care for his birds and eating breakfast.

Initial learning sessions In the beginning, we always review what I've chosen to teach him throughout the day. the next day, he usually studies or learns from 10 a.m. till lunchtime. At these times I am accessible for any inquiries. Each day, we listen to a chapter in a book.

Lunchtime: He takes an extended lunch break that runs from noon until 2 p.m. He enjoys playing video games, therefore he could play some video games in the afternoon too.

Second lesson: Ben studies again from 2 until 4 p.m.

We've discovered that 4 hours of dedicated studying or learning will be sufficient time to complete everything with the exception of 30 minutes.

A lot of families employ a school curriculum, but I've not used one in conjunction with Ben. They are extremely time-consuming and unflexible. I would like a relaxed and comfortable homeschool environment for my child, and would prefer not to replicate private school in my the home. in Chapter 11 I've provided a list of some of the most well-known curriculums that are available to those who are interested in a particular the idea of.

Instead of using a curriculum, we make a list of age-appropriate books and materials which I buy on eBay as well as Amazon. Our schedules have been designed in a different way each year. As Ben was smaller I taught at a modified schedule. In particular, the kindergarten years were filled with playtime: Playdough, coloring, watercolor paints letters using crayons and drawing lines on the paper and lots of reading during the time. The reading would be on the couch, or at night as he was the most popular.

I reading to him three every day, for about 10-20 minutes or more. I would read these young readers to him that we got from the library, till the time came when he was not interested in sitting for long. In the end, I would let him play and run.

The joy of playing and exploring the environment around them is a way to learn for the youngest child. It helps a child improve their motor abilities. Additionally, it aids their brain develop helping with communicating and speaking. My son, who is middle-aged, is a deaf person, and it was easy for me to help teach Ben to sign. The site Signing Time is an outstanding tool to help you with this.

Additionally, for us, teaching and learning was a continuous process. It was not a time to take a vacation during summer. It was much easier to follow a set schedule and be regular. If we did want to travel and we wanted to, we were able to. The only time Ben reached 4th grade when we took a long holiday at Ben's requests, as other kids were allowed to take it. This was fine, but we would read the books to each other all day long whatever. We simply enjoyed it and continues to enjoy it until this day.

If I was reading Ben Ben on a topic regardless of whether it was an engaging fictional story, or a book for children on bugs, rocks and the sun, or dirt, or butterflies I thought about was a form of teaching. (A small suggestion: I discovered used books on eBay which are much less expensive than buying new ones.) Also, I found worksheets and coloring pages on the internet to accompany the books we read. Speaking to Ben gave him a variety of lessons and, perhaps most important was that it helped him learn to read as well as how much he enjoyed reading. I would refer to text while I read and then he would pick the book up. The father would read stories at bedtime to him, too. At the age of five years old, Ben was a great reader. (By this one of the best tips to teach children to read is to turn off the closed captions of the TV.)

Be aware that no two children are created equal like many children do not can grasp math with ease and not all children are able to be readers from an early age, and If that's your child isn't yours, then it's okay. Be who they are. We as parents of children who attend home school don't need to be caught up in scores, lists, or exams (unless you we wish to). In any case, homeschooling gives us space and time to interact in the presence of our children to guide and instruct our children in the manner we feel they should but also to be awed by them and their individuality.

Between the 3rd and 2nd grades We had moved to working with workbooks to learn. I love the printables. Particularly, I discovered and downloaded printables from the web-based source Super Teacher Worksheets.

There is an annual fee, however I found it worth the cost. There are worksheets for the entire spectrum of subjects, an amazing math calculator and art project, as well as history as well as spelling lists and lots more. There are more resources near the end of the book.

As Ben was in the fourth grade, my routine was a mess (I'm employed as a freelancer and do my work at home) So I chose to enroll him in the online school program offered by public schools. Let me tell you that we were both miserable. He didn't seem to learn the most from his year. All he did was click on to the next lesson. I also had to take longer to assist him rather than done the research to help him study by myself. However, in the end the student passed, and we savored our time as the platform came to the close.

In the sixth and fifth grade We reverted to the workbooks, worksheets, and printables. We also did study guides, books as well as some YouTube videos. I put together a playlist for Ben on YouTube We also went to Ted Talks as well. He would then utilize the computer to make notes of what he'd learnt.

In these times We also changed our daily schedule. We devoted less time to books on Mondays and Fridays. This meant that Tuesdays, Wednesdays and Thursdays were a significant day of focus. The plan is to continue this for the second time this year, and but with the possibility of making modifications as our needs change. You could call us an "eclectic" family of homeschoolers. More on this in Chapter 7.

When I began my journey, I was astonished by the fact that "deschooling" as well as "unschooling" are two different things. What do these terms means? In reality, there are many kinds of different ways to learn and teaching at home. In the next sections, we'll explore the different kinds of students, different home-schooling methods and the various homeschooling approaches.

Chapter 17: What Is De Schooling And Game Schooling?

What kind of education at home is best for you? Prior to deciding on the best home schooling style for you You might want to think about "Do you need to eliminate school before we begin?"

What is the definition of deschooling?

Deschooling can be described as a time times, usually weeks and sometimes even months, following the child is no longer in school. parents let their child to be free of the strict school atmosphere and to take a break from their school work. It is important for the child to be able to relax and unwind from the routines of schooling to let them transition into a life at home.

It's not a way to stop the process of learning. It's an opportunity to break away from the strict guidelines which have been set that allow the child to ease into the process and be relaxed, as well as it allows you, as the instructor to relax into the next stage and work out what you're going to achieve. This gives them, as well as you the opportunity to think about the concept of learning and look at new approaches to studying. Learning was once on a computer, but nowadays, your child might be in the kitchen, asking questions on the topic, or asking for clarifications on the new ideas.

You should communicate with your child in regards to this time of deschooling. Tell them why deschooling is important and how long you'll let them take from studying as well as what you'll take over. Make sure they know the expectations and the steps you'll take before you start your own educational plans at home. If you're not sure it's a good idea to organize a discussion with them in order to prioritize and create a plan. This could help your child to be more committed and also become accountable. Honesty and open communication are essential to creating a trustworthy relationship with your child who you be home-educating. If you're not sure about the right answers or aren't certain about something, tell them that you don't know the answer. You can say "I have to consider this a bit more."

There is a chance your child does not know what they should do. They're used to scheduling their day according to a strict schedule. Classes, bells, teachers as well as loads of work might have been their daily routine. Perhaps they quit school due to a difficult issue, for example, an issue with their social life, bullying or lack of a place in normal academics. In these cases it is possible that they need to spend time getting back to their feet and rebuilding confidence.

When you are deschooling it is possible to travel together with the child. Allow them to sleep reading, read with you, cook as they solve puzzles, play games, show them how to fix and repair items, visit the zoo or park as well as visit with relatives, or take in documentaries or movies. Make the most of this time to connect with your children. You'll then be able to send your message to be there for your child. This could be a great opportunity to start teaching gameschooling to the kids.

What exactly is gameschooling?

The game schooling method is based on playing games in order to instruct. It is possible to teach a range of life skills and subjects by using games.

Social capabilities: First the games we play can help us learn the art of winning and losing without a sigh. Nobody likes a grumpy loss or arrogant win. A capacity to lose and win gracefully will benefit children for the rest of their lifetime. The board game allows players to develop their skills in competition and allows the exercise of control. Learning these techniques will allow players to avoid talking about their wins or lamenting about the loss. Learning to teach a child to show respect for the achievements of others is a honed skill. The ability to accept that you have failed about trying hard but having no success, and continuing to try, is a sign of determination.

Skills in reading: Prior to playing the game, there's guidelines to be followed. The rules read aloud can aid all players to be in the same boat and understand the game all in one go. There are many games that have card games "advance" space, and instructions that must be read out loud. A few great games that help develop the ability to read and spell are Scrabble, Mad Libs, Big Boggle, and WordSpiel.

Skills in math: Many board games require exchanging and counting of cash that helps to fine tune multiplying, adding subtracting and multiplying abilities. Games that are great for catching in math abilities comprise Life, Monopoly, Check the Fridge, Yahtzee,

Clumsy Thief as well as Managing My Allowance, to give a couple of examples.

Strategies: Be attentive while thinking critically about the next step is a crucial quality of life. If you make a decision without thinking about it can prove devastating and could cost you your game. While playing, it is a good idea to talk to your kids about how important it is to be patient and considering things so that you can make the best move in the game. This discussion can be correlated with the necessity to make time to consider the implications of the many choices they'll have to make in their daily lives as also. The checkers game, Backgammon, Battleship, and chess are all classic games to practice your "look before you jump" abilities.

Start what you've started -- a crucial ability to live life: completing what you have started is another ability which needs to be cultivated in each of us. In many instances, while playing games or activity, children (or an adult in general!) could want to end the game. As parents, we should encourage our students to stay with what they begin, and to stick with it regardless of the difficulty. The games we play can help us train our minds to become someone who completes whatever they begin.

The gameschooling method can be used to help during summer breaks or for occasions when you require some fresh air. The kids see playing as enjoyable. Have a variety of games available and perhaps create an "game day" in lieu of regular schooling every week. You may want to think about introducing certain games, such as Minecraft as well as Roblox for the development of several of the abilities previously mentioned.

Chapter 18: What Is The Learning Style Of Your Child?

A good understanding of the way your child thinks and learns will make a lot of difference in your efforts to teach them. Don't try to fit the square peg inside the round hole.

Visual learners

They learn by watching. They acquire knowledge through images and reading. Visual cues are used to keep information in mind and to organize their ideas. They are more likely to be drawn by illustrations that include diagrams, maps graphs, charts and other colored flashcards, as well as color-coded objects. They are great at visual pursuits including artwork. They have a tendency to remember phrases, individuals as well as locations. They can also be fascinated by objects as well as the environment around them. They might enjoy watching video clips that show someone walking them through steps in the method. Some people have difficulty following instructions that have not been written out in advance and prefer to be more successful when they have an example of what they're doing.

Auditory learners

Learners learn through being attentive. They must talk about items and understand details verbally in order to absorb details. They do best in situations where stories, instructions as well as assignments are spoken aloud. They are prone to enjoy songs and will sing along while studying or at school. The students learn through repetition descriptions, rhyming and Jingles. They can also be heard talking with others as well as themselves often. As they want being heard can disturb a space. They are known to ask many questions. It's difficult to maintain their focus.

Tactile or kinesthetic learners

They learn through moving by doing and touching. They are generally successful in athletics. They make use of experiences and games to process and retain the information. They might be awed by creating or drawing. They are more likely to enjoy working on projects as well as acting. They should take regular breaks between sitting and studying. The best time to break is at moments if they chew gum or keep things on their hands. (I provided my son with access to the "fidget spinner,"" an exercise ball as well as "slime.") These could also benefit by the use of computers. The kids tend to enjoy hitting buttons.

It is likely that they will be in difficulties in an environment that requires them to break to sit. Instead of structured instruction they may be able to do admirably when presented with a list of work to complete at the time the school day ends. They may surprise you when you give them the ability to finish tasks according to their preferred method. If it does not work, then offer them short training periods and breaks between 15 and 20 minutes, based on their the child's age. Set an alarm for the duration of duration. After that, take a 5 to 10 minute break. Try this 3 or 4 times, and allow for an additional 15 minutes of break after the completion of the work. The strategies can be useful with students who suffer from ADHD.

Students of writing and reading

The students often note down their thoughts and note down their observations. They are able to benefit from revising their notes, and also speaking them aloud. They're self-taught. They love creating reports, essays as well as tales. They enjoy reading and generally are proficient at remembering things they've read. They enjoy spending time at home in peace. They are at their best writing notes of their tasks and appreciate the use of textbooks as well as handouts. They usually have excellent communications skills, and are able to receive what they need from their peers due to this.

Sensory issues in learners

Overstimulation is among the primary reasons why students who suffer from ADHD or autism have trouble. In a classroom that has fluorescent lighting and a teacher who is loud, 20 students who fidget, lots of pictures, posters and papers that are scratching around could be a stressful environment for any person and especially for children with difficulties with sensory processing. The homeschooling option can help a child struggling with sensory issues a more unified learning environment. The parents of such learners are able to make a space that can help students remain in a state of calm and focus.

Some important tips for parents of students with sensory difficulties to think about

1. Check that the learner's seating arrangement is in their favor Consider putting in bands for the chairs to help keep

their feet active. This way, they will be able to be active even when they're in a seated position.

2. A few students may be benefited by the use of a lap pad with weights.

3. Find the best lighting. Lighting is an individual thing that's crucial for people with sensory impairments. If you are able, inquire with your child what light they feel most at ease in. Most likely, it's lighter. Light from the sun may be more desirable.

4. Essential oils such as rosemary or peppermint may increase your alertness. Essential oils like lavender and cedarwood provide a soothing aroma.

5. Some people are sensitive to sounds including music, TV, or even talking are a nuisance and distracting.

Making the most effective learning environment that is conducive to learning for and with your student is crucial. This will pay off watching them grow and develop in their surroundings that are a new and welcoming sensory environment.

Chapter 19: There Are Many Different Styles

Uncoiling

What exactly is unschooling? In general, parents who choose not to school grant their children the ability to decide how they spend their lives, in charge of their learning as well as control over their routines, from when they eat, what time they go to sleep, and even when they wash. They are encouraged by their parents to be free of the things that are natural to their own. There is a variety of levels in this kind of lifestyle. A lot of parents who do not have a schooling program follow guidelines while others do not. There aren't courses or subjects offered that are offered unless the child wants the subject. This is how it works: The children will be able to read if they desire to learn about various topics. The process isn't forced. It's all about what the students want to learn, based on their curiosity, and at their own speed. In the words of a friend, unstructured.

Traditional homeschooling in the traditional way

Utilizing books, curriculums and quizzes, as well as testing and grading, this teaching method brings

from the classroom to your house. The emphasis is on the achievement of students, and the classroom is organized. Grading and record-keeping are important aspects.

Unit studies

This type of study covers subjects for longer periods of time, since the research is more thorough. This is a hands-on method which is a favorite among families who have multiple grade levels. An unit study may involve several subjects. as an example that the spelling of words for the unit corresponds with the animals studying, while the students will be taught about the habitats that the animals inhabit. Our family has personally utilized this approach to learning and have enjoyed using it. Research has also revealed that students who use units study retain up to an average of 45% longer than children employing other methods.

Relaxed home-schooling

They concentrate on the requirements and desires of their child, and use the materials only in situations where they feel necessary. They teach only what they feel is essential for the child's development usually with a non-traditional, hands-on method. They may, however, doubt that their child can be able to learn all the information they require through self-directed learning in the same way as parents who are not educated. The term "unschooling" isn't a reference to unschooling. it's simply a more relaxed way of life which draws knowledge from everyday events. A few home-schoolers are considered "partial unschoolers" because they give their kids as much flexibility as they can to pursue their own pursuits.

Computer-based

There are a variety of online courses designed for parents looking to have an already-established curriculum including step-by-step directions with computer-generated quizzes, tests and records. I've listed a number of these in chapter 11.

Eclectic

This style is a tiny piece of all of it. This is a mix of different styles and methods. We are currently utilizing. Computers are used to teach us how to utilize software programs and create reports using the aid of. While I taught Ben cursive writing and still insist on that he learn it, he doesn't enjoy writing using the pen or pencil. Therefore, when he requires some time away from pencils or pen, he'll opt to "write" using a computer instead. It works well for me.

Like I said previously We also include the unit study into our curriculum. The last time we had an investigation of Milton Hershey. It was a study of geography, history (as we learned quite a bit concerning Hershey, PA), as well as science (the process of making chocolate).

There is a bit of conventional schooling too. We don't take a ton of test taking with Ben I think it's vital for me to know the meanings for a range of terms and also the correct spelling of the word. I send him a daily dictionary and spelling word list. When he is done with the week, I require the child to spell and denote the terms. We also like our Fridays and Mondays to be more laid-back and relaxed, we are more productive on Wednesdays, Tuesdays and Thursdays. We are enthralled by the flexibility schooling at home gives us.

There are various ways of teaching at home but these are only some of the most well-known. It is up to you to determine what is the best option for you and your family. only you know. It's not necessary to have all the answers prior to starting. Simply start! It's an ongoing project which is going to develop a personality on its own. The process will evolve and change and move. There'll be tears, as well as significant achievements. Most important to be aware of is that you're united, and there's a more perfect place than here.

What will my children be Involved in the Society? The Judgment of others

There's no shortage of judgements of other parents regarding homeschooling. Particularly, everybody has a view on how children are educated, and this appears to be on the most prominent of things to judge. The solution to "How are your children educated?" isn't dependent on what others think they should do however, it is based on the way you, as the parent, consider the ideal social experiences are for your child to be like.

Our experience has shown that homeschooling has helped us build more solid bonds with our family. It has been the best outcome from our experience of homeschooling. Thanks to that the fact that our son is able to trust us and relies on us to provide guidance and knowledge regarding the surroundings. He is always there with the questions and worries he has, however, in the modern world the majority of children are developing an unhealthy dependence on their friends. Sure, kids seeking guidance from peers for or to bond with others is not new. However, due to the fact that social media is easy to access, it's happening at more than previously.

Today, relationships with peers are not always good ones and the importance of parents is greater than ever. As the parent, to select the social activities and opportunities your child be exposed to.

To get more insight into this subject, I suggest the book Hold On to Your Children How Parents Must Be More Important than their peers written Written by Gordon Neufeld and Gabor Mate.

The social interaction outside the immediate family group can take many forms:

Playgrounds

Classes in acting

Art classes

Workout/Exercise classes

Co-ops

Dance lessons

Church

Sports for teams, such as basketball, football, baseball as well as soccer (contact the school you attend, since children who are homeschooled are usually allowed to take part in these sports together with children in public schools.) If you have a teenager who is older joining a youth club or even a part-time job can be the ideal way to meet new people. When concerns arise from relatives and acquaintances concerning how you will engage your child in socializing You can say confidently, "I've got this." Be aware that you do not have to make a list that will satisfy their demands can alleviate your anxiety in regards to the judgements of others.

www.ingramcontent.com/pod-product-compliance
Lightning Source LLC
Chambersburg PA
CBHW071442080526
44587CB00014B/1957